Light Years

Light Years

A Girlhood in Hawai'i

by
Susanna Moore

Grove Press
New York

FIRST AMERICAN EDITION

First published in Great Britain in 2007 by Haus Publishing. Originally published as *Lichtjahre, oder Ein Madchen auf Hawaii* in 2006 by marebuchverlag, Hamburg/Germany

ISBN-10: 0-8021-1862-3
ISBN-13: 978-0-8021-1862-2

Grove Press
an imprint of Grove/Atlantic, Inc.
841 Broadway
New York, NY 10003
Distributed by Publishers Group West
www.groveatlantic.com

08 09 10 11 12   10 9 8 7 6 5 4 3 2 1

Contents

.

I

Oh God! For we were all swallowed up in a moment

No memory presents itself of my first acquaintance with the sea. It was always there, and I was always in it.

One summer when my mother was recovering from a breakdown, we lived on the beach at Punalu'u on the north shore of the island of Oah'u. There were five children, of whom I was the eldest. That summer, I was eight years old. My mother was fairly irresistible. She was our leader. We would have jumped into a fire had she wished it. As it was, she had us jumping into the ocean.

I swam in the morning and again in the early afternoon. I swam at sunset. I would swim until I was tired, although not too tired to make it back to the beach. I found a hole in the reef into the deep water at the edge of the channel. If I swam far enough, I could see the big rock on the side of the mountain that marked the site of the shark-god's burial place. Sometimes I was overcome by an inexplicable feeling of panic, as if there were too much beneath and above me. I feared that the ocean might suddenly curl me into a wave and fling me from the loneliness of Earth into the loneliness of space, and I would hurry back through the reef as if the ocean were trying to catch me.

As my mother became less and less rational, I grew convinced that I could see parts of bodies on the clean floor of the ocean. For some time, and to everyone's bafflement, I would not go into the ocean. I spent my time instead with books, quickly exhausting the resources of the small provincial library where I discovered, among other things, that erotic masterpiece about Charles II, *Forever Amber*. I'd been given permission by the amiable librarian, a Samoan woman intent on converting me to Mormonism, to borrow books from the Adults Only shelves after she received a letter from my mother in which my mother duplicitously claimed that the books were for her own use. When I had read all of the library's collection, I was allowed to order books by telephone from a store in downtown Honolulu.

The days were long, as summer days are for children in the countryside, and I found for myself a secret spot where I could read in a grove of coconut palms. The trees were said to have been planted by the King in 1830, and it was a cool and shaded place. There was the sound of the trade wind in the branches, and I could just make out the voices of my brothers and sisters in the water – the constant rush and sweep of the ocean made them sound like angry birds.

In the late afternoon, the men from the neighbourhood would gather on the lawn where they would play music through the night. I'd emerge from the grove each evening, books in hand, dazed and a little sleepy. By the end of the summer, and thanks to Charles Kingsley's *The Water Babies*, I'd returned to the ocean. I never left it again.

I know from my signature in the endpaper of *Robinson Crusoe* that I read it in March of 1954.

I was eight years old, which seems hardly possible except that I recall reading it with great clarity. I was overcome by the idea of shipwreck. I suspect the unconscious was doing its work; my family, while high-strung, was not a shipwreck quite yet, but I divined its coming.

During the winter, we lived in the mountains in Tantalus, a fragrant rain forest, in a large 19th-century shingled house. In place of my palm grove in Punalu'u, I created my version of Crusoe's island, complete with a lean-to made of palm fronds, stocked with old ropes, carefully-rendered maps of hidden treasure and hemp bags of dried fruit and stale bread. I had my own Friday in the form of my younger brother, Rick. It was then that I began to keep a journal about the sea by copying passages from the books I was reading. I began with Defoe, who led me to Stevenson and Conrad, among many others. I was very pleased to discover that Marie Antoinette read the *Journals of Captain Cook* while imprisoned in the Temple.

Hawaii was a ravishing little world. It was an isolated place, redolent with romance. Before the development of jet air-travel in the late 1950s, it had been difficult to reach the Islands – five days by ship from San Francisco (Los Angeles did not exist for us; it was thought to be a little vulgar). It was an hierarchical, snobbish and quietly racist society. This charming, even enchanting life of a mainly *haole* elite was to change, of course, but it lasted for a very long time.

The houses in which I lived were not of spectacular design; most often a vernacular version of a colonial villa, or a house of a simplified New England Greek Revival style with slender columns and a tin roof, or an oversized California bungalow in the Arts and Crafts style, sometimes grand with a screened Greene and Greene sleeping porch and porte cochère like our grey shingled house in Tantalus. Some children, those whose parents were architects or left-wing lawyers who represented longshoremen and other Communists, lived in more modern houses of poured cement and steel, one of which, I remember, was built rather snugly around a large monkeypod tree, suggesting that the growth of the tree had not been sufficiently calculated. Houses at the beach or in the mountains of Wai'anae, or Koke'e on the island of Kaua'i, were made of wood, well-constructed but extremely simple (not in a chic way), indistinguishable but for size from the cottages in the workers' camps built at the turn of the century by Japanese craftsmen, sometimes to sublime effect with carved eaves and porch posts and *tansu*-like cupboards of ohi'a wood. The houses in the mountains had large stone fireplaces; the beach houses and sometimes even the big houses had outdoor showers. Occasionally, a porcelain bathtub was placed in the jungly part of the garden and filled when necessary with rainwater that was stored in large wooden tanks. This water was a rusty reddish-brown color and we used it to wash our hair as well as to bathe. Mainland guests who were unaccustomed to the collecting of rain thought that we chose to wash in dirty water but, out of politeness, never complained, and we did not know to explain. I sometimes worried about the tourists. I did not understand why they had come so far, excluded as they were from the secret and mythical world that I knew, and

I was made anxious by the ease with which they were satisfied – a boat ride around Pearl Harbor to look at the sunken warships and the Kodak Hula Show with dancers in cellophane skirts seemed to suffice. It was the first time that I was to be confused by the difference between what people were willing to accept and what more there was for the taking.

The maids were Japanese; the cook was Chinese, sometimes Filipino. The gardeners were Japanese and the yardmen often the descendants of Portuguese plantsmen from the Azores. Hawaiians were never servants or gardeners; they were sometimes, but rarely, lawyers or doctors or schoolteachers – not because they were discouraged or deterred, but because it held little interest for them. It did not occur to anyone that they wished to be what is called professional, and to all appearances, they didn't.

It took my young mother from Philadelphia, a newcomer then to the Islands, some time to relinquish her East Coast idea of how children ought to look and behave (sterling silver food pushers, like little hoes, to use before a knife was mastered, and tiny correspondence cards engraved with my initials suitable for enclosing with birthday presents). Big rectangular boxes noisy with tissue paper would arrive at the end of August from Best and Co. in New York with seersucker shorts and jackets for the boys, white linen blouses with red rickrack, plaid bathing costumes well elasticized, brown lace-up shoes, navy blue cardigans with faille trim, dresses smocked with little ducks, and piqué sun hats, but she gamely admitted her own particular failure of myth when we eventually rebelled and refused to wear the clothes. At home and when we were not at school, girls wore printed cotton mu'umu'us in unusually bright patterns, and Chinese pajamas with loose trousers, often of shantung or pongee, reaching to the middle of the shin. Twice a year, we were taken downtown to McInerny's where clothes would be laid out for our approval by solemn Japanese saleswomen. The McInernys had been early residents of the islands and had done well, making it all the more thrilling to watch old Miss McInerny boldly stuff girdles, bathing caps, and evening gowns into worn brown paper sacks.

Each night, so we were told, Miss McInerny's maid collected all the things that the old lady had stolen that day and returned them to the store, a system that seemed to please everyone, including us. We wore leis whenever we could (during the Second World War, lei-makers were put to work making camouflage nets), not only on special occasions, and flowers in our hair. Once freed of the Best and Co. boxes, my bathing suits were made for me at Linn's, a small shop on Lewers Avenue, a shaded side street off Kalakaua Avenue in Waikiki. The bathing suit was always the same: two-piece, made of white cotton duck or yellow sharkskin; the bottom not quite a bathing suit but not tennis shorts either, with two vertical rows of buttons that made a flap in front like that on sailors' trousers, and two thin vertical grosgrain stripes down the outside of each leg, usually in navy or red. They were astonishingly smart.

Bicycles were important. We often rode our rusty (the sea air) Schwinns to the old Waialae Country Club for lunch. As the club did not really get busy until the mysteriously named Happy Hour, we were able to commandeer one of the rickety green-felt card cables in the deserted Game Room, consuming egg salad sandwiches and Country Club Ice Tea (the *d* is not used at the end of a word in pidgin; it is 'use cars' and 'barbecue chicken') made with pineapple juice and mint, until we had played a few vicious rounds of greasy cards, at which point I signed the check and we decamped. It would be wildly self-dramatizing to say that we lived off the land, but, depending on the season, we did help ourselves freely (like Captain Cook's Indians) to whatever was growing – mangoes, lichees, tart lady apples, Surinam cherries, *liliko'i*, guavas, oranges, bananas, wild strawberries in patches congested with poison-spewing toads, mint and watercress. There were one or two flowers that were unusually delicious to eat.

There were no fences, no locked gates, no marked boundaries or property lines, and we rode our bikes or roamed unconcerned through woods and plantations – to swim at Jackass Ginger pond in Nu'uanu, it was necessary to pass through many private gardens before reaching the waterfall. Much time, often at night, was spent in the trees, or on the beach, despite the mosquitoes and sand fleas, accompanied by two of our dogs, ungroomed and slightly foul-smelling (the salt water) black poodles, who were not then required to be on leads. We climbed the mountain called Koko Head – once named Kohelepelepe or Vagina Labia Minor – the fire goddess Pele was saved from being raped there by the pig-warrior Kamapua'a when her occasionally loyal sister, Hi'iaka, displayed her vagina to distract him – once innocently breaching the perimeter that a brigade of Marines had established in a war game and, to the curses of the officers, occasioning the failure of the operation.

I kept a large pet spider partly out of affection and partly to eat insects. She sat on my shoulder, retiring under my clothes to sleep. A red thread was tied to one leg (hers) so that I could haul her to safety should I wish to swim or lie down. I finally sat on her, and was somewhat relieved to be rid of her.

My youngest sister was placed eight months after her birth in my wicker bike-basket (lined in blue-and-white *palaka*) and accompanied us on all our jaunts.

It is not an exaggeration to say that until she was two years old she lived by day in the bike-basket. I soon determined that it was too much trouble to pack and to change her cumbersome nappies (especially as there had been talk about the missing gross of diapers that I had tossed into the bushes when soiled), so she was naked. When we'd finished our gallivanting for the day, both she and the wicker basket were briskly hosed down.

I spent my entire childhood and adolescence at the Punahou School in Honolulu, as did all of my friends and my brother. We did not know many children from other schools. There were a few private schools that were Catholic, which meant that mainly Puerto Rican, Portuguese or Filipino children, segregated from us by social class and religion, even if we were Catholic. My second brother was a student at a private boys' school called Iolani. The Kamehameha School, quite a distance from Punahou, held great allure for us. The school had been established in the 19th century by Princess Bernice Pauahi for children of Hawaiian blood. The Kamehameha boys, often very beautiful, and inaccessible to us in a subtle and unspoken way, were splendid athletes. We imagined that they had a familiarity with a sexuality forbidden and even unknown to us, perhaps because of their beauty and grace, but more likely because they were handsome boys with brown skin. We held the Hawaiians in a confused (not articulated or even understood) reverence.

There was a great deal of travel between the islands. This was so, in part, because there were few schools other than Punahou and Kamehameha that took boarders. As a consequence, my friends came from ranches on the Big Island and plantations on Maui and Kaua'i (adults went to Moloka'i only to shoot the slender deer that flourish in the eastern mountains, introduced in 1869 by the Duke of Edinburgh who'd had the deer pressed on him by the Mikado of Japan) and I would go home with them during the long holidays and the summer. I learned to drive when I was thirteen in a surplus World War II Army jeep in the cane fields of Kaua'i – my friend McCully Judd drove an Army tank, destroying beyond redemption

Mrs. Johnson's garden when he lost control of the tank one afternoon. That kind of visiting does not happen much anymore, perhaps because there are more schools on Maui and Hawai'i now.

We were not asked to wear shoes to school until the sixth grade, with the result that I could walk like a fakir over anything, including broken glass. I wore cotton dresses and, when it was very hot, pinafores, the latter causing me much embarrassment until I refused to wear them – I was so convinced that my featureless chest was exposed that I held my arms pressed to my sides, making the use of a blackboard or a baseball bat difficult. We ate lunch in the school cafeteria which was in its own building; it was thought a bit scholar-ship-ish if you carried your lunch to school in a bag or a pail decorated with a cartoon figure. It was possible to sit under a big monkeypod tree in the courtyard – when the tree was in bloom the petals dropped into your food. As at home, the menu was ecumenical – Spam, rice every day, *inari* sushi (which resembled the elbow skin of an old Japanese man), chicken *hekka*, tuna on damp white bread, *char siu* pork, Portuguese sausage, macaroni salad (known as mac), *malasadas* (sweet lumpy Portuguese doughnuts without holes), kimchee, Fritos, saimin (noodle soup), beef teriyaki on bamboo sticks.

I was passionate about my teachers. Some of them were shockingly young (it was rumored that in the upper school, known as the Academy, there was clandestine dating between some of the girls and the teachers – as a student in the Academy myself one day I can confirm that there was), in their early twenties, often from the East Coast, and I wonder if Honolulu was not a particularly good place to spend a year or two after leaving Yale and before moving on to a more suitable career (Viet Nam). In the second grade, I asked my teacher, Mrs. Corcoran, to have lunch with me one Saturday at the old Moana Hotel in Waikiki, signing my name to the check in a large left-handed scrawl. I have wondered why she agreed to go. I kept it a secret for many years. My fifth-grade teacher, a very attractive gentleman fresh from Williams, was, to my great distress, lost one summer taking a dugout up the Sepik River in Papua New Guinea.

After school, we would leave the grounds through the lower gate covered with night-blooming cereus (which we did not see in bloom until we were much older, being asleep in our beds by the hour that the big, waxy flowers deigned to open) to buy penny candy, preserved seeds of mango, plum, and cherry called *see moi*, and white paper cones of shaved ice flavored with artificial syrups in fluorescent colors at a tiny grocery. The store, called the Chink Store because of our unquestioned devotion to the Chinese husband and wife who owned it, had been patronized by Punahou children for generations. Away from school, I was sometimes chased by terrifying local girls called *titas* (from the Portuguese for 'aunt') who, for sport, did not take to *haoles* – the excuse for a chase was usually the absurd accusation that I had been staring at them. The signal for me to run was when one of them shouted loudly, 'What? I owe you money?'

Once a week, I attended cotillion at the Royal Hawaiian Hotel, held in a longhouse in the hotel's then enormous garden. I was once required to leave in disgrace for surreptitiously turning on the fire-prevention sprinkling system concealed in the thatch roof (I was caught because I was the only one not drenched to the skin) and ruining everyone's painful patent leather pumps, and once I was asked to leave for secreting a hat pin in my white cotton glove, the better to prick the balloon decorations, thus causing our instructor, the red-haired Mrs. Wallace, to fall to the ground holding her bosom as if shot. The classes, although sweaty, were useful in the end. I and my dazed partner (it was a far worse experience for boys) bumped across the polished floor in stiff but enthusiastic renditions of the box step, later to be revealed as the fox-trot by the amused older men I began to dance with when I was fifteen, usually at weddings.

I did not have many possessions. For some time, I was bewitched by a wooden dollhouse; a chalet from Switzerland, complete with tiny red velvet geraniums in pots and a clean cow barn with minuscule bundles of straw and threadlike brown leather halters hanging on painted hooks. A cloth doll from Jamaica with gold earrings and a bright red cotton head wrap, the kind of curio sold on cruise ships, held my attention for quite some time. I played with the doll and the house, wildly mismatched and the doll three times the size of the house, for perhaps too long, but I had little other than an endless supply of books, which was literally my salvation.

DANIEL DEFOE, from Robinson Crusoe

Our ship was about 120 ton burthen; carried six guns and fourteen men, besides the master, his boy, and myself. We had on board no large cargo of goods, except of such toys as were fit for our trade with the negroes – such as beads, bits of glass, shells and odd trifles, especially little looking-glasses, knives, scissors, hatchets, and the like.

The same day I went on board we set sail, standing away to the northward upon our own coast, with design to stretch over for the African coast when they came about 10 or 12 degrees of northern latitude; which, it seems, was the manner of their course in those days. We had very good weather, only excessively hot, all the way upon our own coast, till we came the height of Cape St. Augustino; from whence, keeping farther off at sea, we lost sight of land, and steered as if we were bound for the Isle Fernande de Noronha, holding our course north-east by north, and leaving those isles on the east. In this course we passed the line in about twelve days' time; and were by our last observation in 7 degrees 22 minutes northern latitude, when a violent tornado or hurricane took us quite out of our knowledge. It began from the south-east, came about to the north-west, and then settled into the north-east; from whence it blew in such a terrible manner that for twelve days together we could do nothing but drive, and, scudding away before it, let it carry us whither ever fate and the fury of the winds directed. And during these twelve days I need not say that I expected every day to be swallowed up; nor, indeed, did any in the ship expect to save their lives.

19

In this distress, we had, besides the terror of the storm, one of our men died of the calenture, and one man and the boy washed overboard. About the twelfth day, the weather abating a little, the master made an observation as well as he could, and found that he was in about 11 degrees north latitude, but that he was 22 degrees of longitude difference west from Cape St. Augustino; so that he found he was gotten upon the coast of Guiana, or the north part of Brazil, beyond the River Amazones, toward that of the River Oronoque, commonly called the Great River, and began to consult with me what course he should take, for the ship was leaky and very much disabled, and he was going directly back to the coast of Brazil.

I was positively against that; and looking over the charts of the seacoast of America with him, we concluded there was no inhabited country for us to have recourse to till we came within the circle of the Carribbe Islands, and therefore resolved to stand away for Barbadoes; which, by keeping off at sea, to avoid the indraught of the Bay or Gulf of Mexico, we might easily perform, as we hoped, in about fifteen days' sail; whereas we could not possibly make our voyage to the coast of Africa without some assistance both to our ship and to ourselves.

With this design we changed our course, and steered away north-west by west, in order to reach some of our English islands, where I hoped for relief. But our voyage was otherwise determined; for, being in the latitude of 12 degrees 18 minutes, a second storm came upon us, which carried us away with the same impetuosity westward, and drove us so out of the very way of all human commerce, that had all our lives been saved as to the sea, we were rather in danger of being devoured by savages than ever returning to our own country.

In this distress, the wind still blowing very hard, one of our men early in the morning cried out, 'Land!' and we had no sooner run out of the cabin to look out in hopes of seeing whereabouts in the world we were, but the ship struck upon a sand, and in a moment, her motion being so stopped, the sea broke over her in such a manner, that we expected we should all have perished immediately, and we were immediately driven into our close quarters to shelter us from the very foam and spray of the sea.

It is not easy for anyone who has not been in the like condition to describe or conceive the consternation of men in such circumstances. We knew nothing where we were, or upon what land it was we were driven, whether an island or the main, whether inhabited or not inhabited; and as the rage of the wind was still great, though rather less than at first, we could not so much as hope to have the ship hold many minutes without breaking in pieces, unless the winds by a kind of miracle should turn immediately about. In a word, we sat looking one upon another, and expecting death every moment, and every man acting accordingly as preparing for another world, for there was little or nothing more for us to do in this. That which was our present comfort, and all the comfort we had, was that contrary to our expectation, the ship did not break yet, and that the master said the wind began to abate.

Now, though we thought that the wind did a

little abate, yet the ship having thus struck upon the sand, and sticking too fast for us to expect her getting off, we were in a dreadful condition indeed, and had nothing to do but to think of saving our lives as well as we could. We had a boat at our stern just before the storm, but she was first staved by dashing against the ship's rudder, and in the next place she broke away, and either sunk or was driven off to sea; so there was no hope from her. We had another boat on board, but how to get her off into the sea was a doubtful thing. However, there was no room to debate, for we fancied the ship would break in pieces every minute, and some told us she was actually broken already.

In this distress the mate of our vessel layed hold of the boat, and with the help of the rest of the men they got her slung over the ship's side, and getting all into her, let go, and committed ourselves, being eleven in number, to God's mercy and the wild sea: for though the storm was abated considerably, yet the sea went dreadfully high upon the shore, and might well be called 'den wild zee', as the Dutch call the sea in a storm.

And now our case was very dismal indeed; for we all saw plainly that the sea went so high that the boat could not live, and that we should be inevitably drowned. As to making sail, we had none; nor, if we had, could we have done anything with it: so we worked at the oar towards the land, though with heavy hearts, like men going to execution; for we all knew that when the boat came nearer the shore she would be dashed in a thousand pieces by the breach of the sea. However, we committed our souls to God in the most earnest manner, and the wind driving us towards the shore we hastened our destruction with our own hands, pulling as well as we could towards land.

What the shore was – whether rock or sand, whether steep or shoal – we knew not; the only hope that could rationally give us the least shadow of expectation was, if we might happen into some bay or gulf, or the mouth of some river, where by great chance we might have run our boat in, or got under the lee of the land, and perhaps made smooth water. But there was nothing of this appeared; but as we made nearer and nearer the shore, the land looked more frightful than the sea.

After we had rowed or rather driven about a league and a half, as we reckoned it, a raging wave, mountain-like, came rolling astern of us, and plainly bade us expect the *coup-de-grace*. In a word, it took us with such a fury, that it overset the boat at once, and, separating us as well from the boat as from one another, gave us not time hardly to say, O God! For we were all swallowed up in a moment.

Nothing can describe the confusion of thought which I felt when I sunk into the water, for though I swam very well, yet I could not deliver myself from the waves so as to draw breath, till that a wave, having driven me or rather carried me a vast way on towards the shore, and having spent itself, went back, and left me upon the land almost dry, but half-dead with the water I took in. I had so much presence of mind as well as breath left that, seeing myself nearer the mainland than I expected, I got upon my feet, and endeavoured to make on towards the land as fast as I could before another wave should return and take me up again.

But I soon found it was impossible to avoid it; for I saw the sea come after me as high as a great hill, and as furious as an enemy which I had no means or strength to contend with. My business was to hold my breath and rise myself upon the water if I could, and so by swimming to preserve my breathing and pilot myself towards the shore if possible; my greatest concern now being that the sea, as it would carry me a great way towards the shore when it came on, might not carry me back again with it when it gave back towards the sea.

The wave that came upon me again buried me at once twenty or thirty feet deep in its own body; and I could feel myself carried with a mighty force and swiftness towards the shore a very great way; but I held my breath, and assisted myself to swim still forward with all my might. I was ready to burst with holding my breath, when, as I felt myself rising up, so to my immediate relief I found my head and hands shoot out above the surface of the water; and though it was not two seconds of time that I could keep myself so, yet it relieved me greatly, gave me breath and new courage. I was covered again with water a good while, but not so long but I held it out; and finding the water had spent itself and began to return, I struck forward against the return of the waves, and felt ground again with my feet. I stood still a few moments to recover breath, and till the water went from me, and then took to my heels and ran with what strength I had farther towards the shore. But neither would this deliver me from the fury of the sea, which came pouring in after me again, and twice more I was lifted up by the waves and carried forwards as before, the short being very flat.

The last time of these two had well near been fatal to me; for the sea, having hurried me along as before, landed me, or rather dashed me against a piece of rock, and that with such force, as it left me senseless, and indeed helpless as to my own deliverance: for the blow taking my side and breast, beat the breath as it were quite out of my body, and had it returned again immediately, I must have been strangled in the water; but I recovered a little before the return of the waves, and seeing I should be covered again with the water, I resolved to hold fast by a piece of the rock, and so to hold my breath, if possible, till the wave went back. Now as the waves were not so high as at first, being near land, I held my hold till the wave abated, and then fetched another run, which brought me so near the shore, that the next wave, though it went over me, yet did not so swallow me up as to carry me away; and the next run I took I got to the mainland, where, to my great comfort, 1 clambered up the cliffs of the shore and sat me down upon the grass, free from danger, and quite out of the reach of the water.

JOHN FISKE, from
The Discovery of America

At length, on the 6th of September, (Columbus) set sail from Gomera, but were becalmed and had made only thirty miles by the night of the 8th. The breeze then freshened, and when next day the shores of Ferro, the last of the Canaries, sank from sight on the eastern horizon, many of the sailors loudly lamented their unseemly fate, and cried and sobbed like children. Columbus well understood the difficulty of dealing with these men. He provided against one chief source of discontent by keeping two different reckonings, a true one for himself and a false one for his officers and crews. He was shrewd enough not to overdo it and awaken distrust. Thus after a twenty-four hours' run of 180 miles on September 10, he reported it as 144 miles; next day the run was 120 miles and he announced it as 108, and so on. But for this prudent if somewhat questionable device, it is not unlikely that the first week of October would have witnessed a mutiny in which Columbus would have been either thrown overboard or forced to turn back.

The weather was delicious, and but for the bug-a-boos that worried those poor sailors it would have been a most pleasant voyage. Chief among the imaginary terrors were three which deserve especial mention. At nightfall on September 13 the ships had crossed the magnetic line of no variation, and Columbus was astonished to see that the compass-needle, instead of pointing a little to the right of the pole-star, began to sway toward the left, and next day this deviation increased. It was impossible to hide such a fact from the sharp eyes of the pilots, and all were seized with alarm at the suspicion that this witch instrument was beginning to play them some foul trick in punishment of their temerity; but Columbus was ready with an ingenious astronomical explanation, and their faith in the profundity of his knowledge prevailed over their terrors.

The second alarm came on September 16, when they struck into vast meadows of floating seaweeds and grasses, abounding in tunny fish and crabs. They had now come more than 800 miles from Ferro and were entering the wonderful Sargasso Sea, that region of the Atlantic six times as large as France, where vast tangles of vegetation grow upon the surface of water that is more than 2,000 fathoms deep, and furnish sustenance for an untold wealth of fishy life. To the eye of the mariner the Sargasso Sea presents somewhat the appearance of an endless green prairie, but modern ships plow through it with ease and so did the caravels of Columbus at first. After two or three days, however, the wind being light, their progress was somewhat impeded. It was not strange that the crews were frightened at such a sight. It seemed uncanny and weird, and revived ancient fancies about mysterious impassable seas and overbold mariners whose ships had been stuck fast in them. The more practical spirits were afraid of running aground upon submerged shoals, but all were somewhat reassured on this point when it was found that their longest plummet-lines failed to find bottom.

On September 22 the journal reports 'no more grass'. They were in clear water again, and more than 1,400 geographical miles from the Canaries. A third source of alarm had already begun to disturb the sailors. They were discovering much more than they had bargained for. There were in the belt of the trade winds, and as the gentle but unfailing breeze wafted them steadily westward, doubts began to arise as to whether it would ever be possible to return. Fortunately soon after this question began to be discussed, the wind, jealous of its character for capriciousness even there, veered into the southwest.

By September 25, the Admiral's chief difficulty had come to be the impatience of his crews at not finding land. On that day there was a mirage, or some such illusion, which Columbus and all hands supposed to be a coast in front of them, and hymns of praise were sung, but at dawn next day they were cruelly undeceived. Flights of strange birds and other signs of land kept raising hopes which were presently dashed again, and the men passed through alternately hot and cold fits of exultation and dejection. Such mockery seemed to show that they were entering a realm of enchantment. Somebody, perhaps one of the released jail-birds, hinted that if a stealthy thrust should happen some night to push the Admiral overboard, it could be plausibly said that he had slipped and fallen while star-gazing. His situation grew daily more perilous, and the fact that he was an Italian commanding Spaniards did not help him. Perhaps what saved him was their vague belief in his superior knowledge; they may have felt that they should need him in going back,

By October 4 there were ominous symptoms of

mutiny, and the anxiety of Columbus was evinced in the extent of his bold understatement of that day's run, – 138 miles instead of the true figure 189. For some days his pilots had been begging him to change his course; perhaps they had passed between islands. Anything for a change! On the 7th at sunrise, they had come 2,724 geographical miles from the Canaries, which was farther than the Admiral's estimate of the distance to Cipango; but according to his false statement of the runs, it appeared that they had come scarcely 2,200 miles ... the temper of the sailors was growing more dangerous with every mile, – until October 11, when the signs of land became unmistakable, and the wildest excitement prevailed. A reward of 10,000 maravedis had been promised to the person who should first discover land, and ninety pairs of eyes were strained that night with looking. About ten o'clock the Admiral, standing on the tower-like poop of his vessel, saw a distant light moving as if somebody were running along the shore with a torch. This interpretation was doubted, but a few hours later a sailor on the *Pinta* saw land distinctly, and soon it was visible to all, a long low coast about five miles distant. This was at two in the morning of Friday, October 12, – just ten weeks since they had sailed from Palos, just thirty-three days since they had lost sight of the coast of Ferro. The sails were now taken in, and the ships lay to, awaiting the dawn.

SANTO BLANCO, from
The Last of the Seris

'The Song of the Whale'

I am large and very strong
I am swift through the water.
Because of my speed I fear nothing.
No shark can catch me.

The sea is calm
there is no wind.
In the warm sun

I play on the surface
with many companions.
In the air spout
many clouds of smoke
and all of them are happy.

The mother whale is happy.
She swims on the surface, very fast.
No shark is near
but she swims over many leagues back and
    forth, very fast.
Then she sinks to the bottom and four
    baby whales are born.

First one comes up to the surface
in front of her nose.
He jumps on the surface.
Then each of the other baby whales
jumps on the surface.
Then they go down
into the deep water to their mother
and stay there eight days
before they come up again.

The old, old whale has no children
She does not swim far.
She floats near the shore and is sad.
She is so old and weak
she cannot feed like other whales.
With her mouth on the surface
she draws in her breath – hrrr –
and the smallest fish and the sea birds are
    swallowed up.

The whale coming to shore is sick
the sharks have eaten her bowels
and the meat of her body.
She travels slowly – her bowels are gone.
She is dead on the shore
and can travel no longer.

Fifty sharks surrounded her.
They came under her belly
and bit off her flesh and her bowels
and so she died. Because she had no teeth
to fight the sharks.

PO CHU-YI, from Sunflower Splendor

'Ripples Sifting Sand'

1

How can the tide of the river be compared
    to your love?
Or the waters of the sea to a woman's heart?
Missing you, I'd rather have the tide that
    keeps its promise;
Longing for you, I begin to realize the
    ocean is not as deep.

2

There'll be a day when dust flies at the
    bottom of the sea.
And the time will come for the
    mountainside to crumble into stones.
Who'd know that when a young lover casts
    aside his woman,
Once he has boarded a boat, there is no
    date of his return.

II

One knows not what sweet mystery about this sea

The long white crescent of Waikiki Beach was crowded with both tourists and local people in 1960 – nowadays there are mostly tourists on the beach. Outrigger canoes belonging to the different racing clubs once lined the shore. When the waves were high enough – surfing was never particularly good at Waikiki – the canoes, with four or five pale-skinned paying customers and a beachboy as steersman, would be taken out for canoe-surfing. It was a surprisingly exciting ride as the stern of the canoe would often be lifted high, the speed of the canoe outpacing the speed the wave, causing it to overturn itself stern to bow, in a mishap known as pearl-diving. It is not dangerous in those calm waters, and because of the floating *ama*, or outrigger, it only

39

required its occupants to turn the canoe right-side-up. You then hoisted yourself over the side to bail with the coffee can kept in the bottom of the canoe for that purpose, assuming the can had not floated away.

Sometimes we were taken to Kuhio Beach, at the far western end, the Diamond Head end of the bay. It was not a fashionable beach, frequented by noisy, sometimes rough local kids. In Kapiolani Park, which begins at the edge of Kuhio Beach, old Chinese men gambled at dominos and the handsome Hawaiian boys gathered under the palms to tease the passing girls. There was a short quay at Kuhio and a cement breakwater which rendered the ocean rather tepid in temperature, and very shallow. The sandy bottom was undisturbed by coral, or even shells.

The beaches away from Waikiki were empty but for the occasional badly sunburned enlisted boys from the mainland in inappropriate bathing shorts who had wandered innocently into the dangerous surf on a quick round-the-island jaunt. By 1970, however, the pale Japanese girls could no longer be kept at home by old-fashioned parents. They were still very

Japanese with their neat ponytails and baskets of sunscreen and lip salve. They kept apart, but the very fact that they were watching their boyfriends in the surf made me wonder where they had been all those years when my friends and I had been the only ones on the beach. Perhaps they'd been in sewing class or Japanese language school. I could not imagine what their grandmothers thought of them. It was an early lesson in the conflict of democratization.

If there were ten Japanese girls lying on the beach, there were ten fewer Japanese girls who still wore kimono and *geta*, who knew how to play the *samisen*, and arrange cherry blossoms in a way no *haole* could ever devise – but was that too a myth? The playing of the *samisen* was unknown to these girls' grandmothers, who had been brought to Hawai'i to labor in the fields. They could not resort to any instrument after twelve hours in the pineapple fields, their fingers horribly slashed. I wondered if it were a wonderful, if inevitable thing to wear a pink gingham bikini rather than a hobbled silk robe. Although a Mrs. Gerould wrote in 1923 that 'it is impossible to be afraid of any one who wears a kimono, and that fact may be either our salvation or our undoing in our relations with the Orient,' it could no longer be said that the most sensual part of a Japanese woman was the nape of her neck.

On the weekends, we went into the mountains, depending on the season, to pick ginger and to dig up rare ferns to grow in pots, and to float down the flumes, absolutely forbidden to us, that carried the cold mountain water that irrigated the pineapple and cane fields. The wooden flumes, often on trestles and sometimes running underground, were lined with leeches that I picked from my bare legs and shirtsleeves when I emerged breathless from the chute. There was a myth that you would be chopped to pieces by the metal blades of a waterwheel should you not remove yourself from the flume in time – oddly enough this was said to have happened only to Japanese girls, suggesting that they were not so agile; not so thoroughly island girls as ourselves. I twice broke my wrist (the same wrist) fluming. The second time I was afraid to tell my father, who was a doctor, because he had warned me to be careful until my first fracture had healed. I made a cast for myself in the garage out of wet newspapers and paste and went in to supper and vomited on the table.

If it had been raining, we went *ti*-leaf sliding down the muddy and precipitous ditches made by the ancient Hawaiians for sledding called *he'e holua* (the dangerous slides are now abandoned; the Visitors Bureau put telephone poles midway down each slide to discourage tourists after one of then was killed – what was he doing there in the first place? we asked indignantly), or to the beach, either to the Outrigger Canoe Club which was private and then in the center of Waikiki, next to the Royal Hawaiian Hotel, or to Sandy Beach, or Makapu'u Beach at the eastern point of O'ahu where one of the goddess Pele's petroglyphs sat high on the hill, overlooking the bay.

Punalu'u is the district known to be the haunt of the god Kamapua'a who, before Freud but after Herodotus, could take the shape of a pig or a handsome man – while a pig, he destroyed the lands of the *ali'i*; while a man, he seduced their women. 'Leaving his horse at the termination of the valley and entering this narrow pass of not over fifty or sixty feet in width, the traveller winds his way along, crossing and recrossing the stream several times, till he seems to be entering into the very mountain ... One is stopped by a wall of solid rock rising perpendicularly ... to the height of some two hundred feet, and down which the whole stream must have descended in a beautiful fall ... The smooth channels are said to have been made by [Kamapua'a] ... Old natives still believe that they are the prints of his back. A party who recently visited the spot states that when they reached the falls they were instructed to make an offering ... This was done in true Hawaiian style; they built a tiny pile of stones on one or two large leaves, and so made themselves safe from falling stones, which otherwise would assuredly have struck them.'

One summer, my brother Rick, who was then twelve years old, stayed at Punalu'u with Dr. Welles and his family in a large house on the beach. Dr. Welles, who was part Hawaiian, and his *haole* wife, had managed to hold fast to a part of old Hawai'i. In the first light (sometimes in the dark with torches), we searched for any blue-glass balls that might have broken free from fishing nets in the Sea of Japan to float heedlessly across the Pacific to wash ashore at high tide. During the day, we collected *limu* (seaweed) and went spearfishing and prized *opihi* (tiny snails) from the ledges of the rock pools. It was not only in occupation and food that the Welles were old-fashioned, but in their *ho'okipa*, or generosity. We ate at a long wooden table on the lawn. It was impossible to know how many places to set until the last moment – often there were twenty people for dinner. Late at night, the *pune'es* and *hickie'es*, sleeping platforms that had been used as sofas during the day, were transformed into beds with the addition of pillows and light straw mats or quilts (no sheets) for any guests who chose to stay the night or could not make it home.

Early each evening, the Hawaiians who lived nearby strolled across the lawn with their bottles of *okolehao* (homemade swipe most often made from fermented pineapple) and ukuleles and guitars. Most of the Hawaiian men that we knew worked for the city and county repairing the roads, or as entertainers at the clubs and hotels in town, or as small subsistence farmers and fishermen. (One of my Hawaiian friends insisted that Hawaiians were not working class. The working class wanted televisions and motorboats, but Hawaiians didn't want anything.) The sun had not yet gone down, and the men and children carried chairs and wooden benches onto the lawn. Among the men was the musician Gabby Pahinu'i, who worked on the road crew. There was beer, and reeking cuttlefish, and sashimi. After a few hours of talking-story, Pahinu'i would play slack-key guitar. He sang in Hawaiian and the other men played with him; some of the women, one at a time, rose to dance hula on the grass. The singing and dancing lasted through the night. 'We have several times been kept awake by the natives ... talking and singing till near daybreak. Circumstances the most trivial sometimes furnish conversation for hours. Their songs also afford much amusement ... It is probable that many of the fabulous tales and songs so popular among them, have originated in the gratification they find in thus spending their time,' wrote the missionary William Ellis in 1823.

I awoke on the grass in the morning, rolled in a mat damp with dew. The men had gone to work. Dr. Welles was at the clinic. I would wash in the outdoor shower, and my brother and I would go fishing. I was aware that while I didn't yet understand what it meant to be attached to this Earth, I did not want to make the mistake of imagining that myth was something available to everyone. I understood that myth was a luxury.

HERMAN MELVILLE, from Moby Dick

Chapter 111, 'The Pacific'

When gliding by the Bashee isles we emerged at last upon the great South Sea; were it not for other things, I could have greeted my dear Pacific with uncounted thanks, for now the long supplication of my youth was answered; that serene ocean rolled eastwards from me a thousand leagues of blue.

There is, one knows not what sweet mystery about this sea, whose gently awful stirrings seem to speak of some hidden soul beneath; like those fabled undulations of the Ephesian sod over the buried Evangelist St. John. And meet it is, that over these sea-pastures, wide-rolling watery prairies and Potters' Fields of all four continents, the waves should rise and fall, and ebb and flow unceasingly; for here, millions of mixed shades and shadows, drowned dreams, somnambulisms, reveries; all that we call lives and souls, lie dreaming, dreaming, still; tossing like slumberers in their beds; the ever-rolling waves but made so by their restlessness.

To any meditative Magian rover, this serene Pacific, once beheld, must ever after be the sea of his adoption. It rolls the midmost waters of the world, the Indian ocean and Atlantic being but its arms. The same waves wash the moles of the new-built California towns, but yesterday planted by the recentest race of men, and lave the faded but still gorgeous skirts of Asiatic lands, older than Abraham; while all between float milky-ways of coral isles, and low-lying, endless, unknown Archipelagoes, and impenetrable Japans. Thus this mysterious, divine Pacific zones the world's whole bulk about; makes all coasts one bay to it, seems the tide-beating heart of earth. Lifted by those eternal swells. you needs must own the seductive god, bowing your head to Pan.

But few thoughts of Pan stirred Ahab's brain, as standing like an iron statue at his accustomed place beside the mizen rigging, with one nostril he unthinkingly snuffed the sugary musk from the Bashee isles (in whose sweet woods mild lovers must be walking), and with the other consciously inhaled the salt breath of the new found sea; that sea in which the hated White Whale must even then be swimming. Launched at length upon these almost final waters, and gliding towards the Japanese cruising-ground, the old man's purpose intensified itself. His firm lips met like the lips of a vice; the Delta of his forehead's veins swelled like overladen brooks; in his very sleep, his ringing cry ran through the vaulted hull, 'Stem all! the White Whale spouts thick blood!'

CHARLES DARWIN, *from*
The Voyage of the Beagle

After having been detained six days in Wigwam Cove
by very bad weather, we put to sea on the 30th of
December. Captain Fitz Roy wished to get westward
to land York and Fuegia in their own country. When
at sea we had a constant succession of gales, and the
current was against us: we drifted to 57 degrees 23'
south. On the 11th of January, 1833, by carrying a
press of sail, we fetched within a few miles of the
great rugged mountain of York Minster (so called
by Captain Cook, and the origin of the name of the
elder Fuegian), when a violent squall compelled us
to shorten sail and stand out to sea. The surf was
breaking fearfully on the coast, and the spray was
carried over a cliff estimated at 200 feet in height.
On the 12th the gale was very heavy, and we did not
know exactly where we were: it was a most unpleasant
sound to hear constantly repeated, 'keep a good lookout to leeward'. On the 13th the storm raged with
its full fury: our horizon was narrowly limited by the

sheets of spray borne by the wind. The sea looked ominous, like a dreary waving plain with patches of drifted snow: whilst the ship laboured heavily, the albatross glided with its expanded wings right up the wind. At noon a great sea broke over us, and filled one of the whale-boats, which was obliged to be instantly cut away. The poor *Beagle* trembled at the shock, and for a few minutes would not obey her helm; but soon, like a good ship that she was, she righted and came up to the wind again. Had another sea followed the first, our fate would have been decided soon, and for ever. We had not been twenty-four days trying in vain to get westward; the men were worn out with fatigue, and they had not for many nights or days a dry thing to put on. Captain Fitz Roy gave up the attempt to get westward by the outside coast. In the evening we ran in behind False Cape Horn, and dropped our anchor in forty-seven fathoms, fire flashing from the windlass as the chain rushed round it. How delightful was that still night, after having been so long involved in the din of the warring elements!

JULIAN CORBETT, from **Sir Francis Drake**

So protected, Drake boldly entered the Straits. Then from the towering snowcones and threatening glaciers that guarded the entry the tempests swept down upon the daring intruders. Out of the tortuous gulfs that through the bowels of the fabulous Austral continent seemed to lead beyond the confines of the world, rude squalls buffeted them this way and that, and currents, the like of which no man had seen, made as though they would dash them to pieces in the fathomless depths where no cable would reach. Fires lit by natives on the desolate shore as the strangers straggled by, added the terrors of unknown magic. But Drake's fortitude and consummate seamanship triumphed over all, and in a fortnight he brought his ill-sailing ships in triumph out upon the Pacific. Then, as though maddened to see how the adventurers had braved every effort to destroy them, the whole fury of the fiends that guarded the South Sea's slumber rushed howling upon them. Hardly had the squadron turned northward than a terrific gale struck at it and hurled it back. The sky was darkened, and the bowels of the earth seemed to have burst, and for nearly two months they were driven under bare poles to and fro without rest in latitudes where no ship had ever sailed. On the maps the great Austral continent was marked, but they found in its place an enchanted void, where wind and water, and ice and darkness, seemed to make incessant war. After three weeks' strife, the *Marygold* went down with all hands; and in another week Wynter lost heart, and finding himself at the mouth of the Straits, went home in despair; while the *Golden Hind*, ignorant of the desertion, was swept once more to the south of Cape Horn. Here, on the fifty-third day of its fury, the storm ceased exhausted, and Drake found himself alone. But it was no moment to repine, for he knew he had made a discovery so brilliant as to deprive even Magellan's of its radiance. He was anchored among islands southward of anything known to geographers, and before him the Atlantic and Pacific rolled together in one great flood. In his exultation he landed on the farthest island, and walking alone with his instruments to its end, he laid himself down, and with his arms embraced the southern-most point of the known world.

JOSEPH CONRAD, from Typhoon

Observing the steady fall of the barometer, Captain MacWhirr thought. 'There's some dirty weather knocking about.' This is precisely what he thought. He had had an experience of moderately dirty weather – the term dirty as applied to the weather implying only moderate discomfort to the seaman. Had he been informed by an indisputable authority that the end of the world was to be finally accomplished by a catastrophic disturbance of the atmosphere, he would have assimilated the information under the simple idea of dirty weather, and no other, because he had no experience of cataclysms, and belief does not necessarily imply comprehension. The wisdom of his country had pronounced by means of an Act of Parliament that before he could be considered as fit to take charge of a ship he should be able to answer certain simple questions on the subject of circular storms such as hurricanes, cyclones, typhoons; and apparently he had answered them, since he was now in command of the *Nan-Shan* in the China seas during the season of typhoons. But if he had answered he remembered nothing of it. He was, however, conscious of being made uncomfortable by the clammy heat. He came out on the bridge, and found no relief to this oppression. The air seemed thick. He gasped like a fish, and began to believe himself greatly out of sorts.

The *Nan-Shan* was ploughing a vanishing furrow upon the circle of the sea that had the surface and the shimmer of an undulating piece of gray silk. The sun, pale and without rays, poured down leaden heat in a strangely indecisive light, and the Chinamen were lying prostrate about the decks. Their bloodless, pinched, yellow faces were like the faces of bilious invalids. Captain MacWhirr noticed two of them especially, stretched out on their backs below the bridge. As soon as they had closed their eyes they seemed dead. Three others, however, were quarrelling barbarously away forward; and one big fellow, half naked, with herculean shoulders, was hanging limply over a winch; another, sitting on the deck, his knees up and his head drooping sideways in a girlish attitude, was plaiting his pigtail with infinite languor depicted in his whole person and in the very movement of his fingers. The smoke struggled with difficulty out of the funnel, and instead of streaming away spread itself out like an infernal sort of cloud, smelling of sulphur and raining soot all over the decks.

'What the devil are you doing there. Mr. Jukes?' asked Captain MacWhirr.

This unusual form of address, though mumbled rather than spoken, caused the body of Mr. Jukes to start as though it had been prodded under the fifth rib. He had had a low bench brought on the bridge, and sitting on it with a length of rope curled about his feet and a piece of canvas stretched over his knees, was pushing a sail-needle vigorously. He looked up, and his surprise gave to his eyes an expression of innocence and candour.

'I am only roping some of that new set of bags we made last trip for whipping up coals,' he remonstrated, gently. 'We shall want them for the next coaling, sir.'

'What became of the others?'

'Why, worn out of course, sir.'

Captain MacWhirr, after glaring down irresolutely at his chief mate, disclosed the gloomy and cynical conviction that more than half of them had been lost overboard, 'if only the truth was known,' and retired to the other end of the bridge. Jukes, exasperated by this unprovoked attack, broke the needle at the second stitch, and dropping his work got up and cursed the heat in a violent undertone.

The propeller thumped, the three Chinamen forward had given up squabbling very suddenly, and the one who had been plaiting his tail clasped his legs and stared dejectedly over his knees, The lurid sunshine cast faint and sickly shadows. The swell ran higher and swifter every moment, and the ship lurched heavily in the smooth, deep hollows of the sea.

'I wonder where that beastly swell comes from,' said Jukes aloud, recovering himself after a stagger.

'North-east,' grunted the literal MacWhirr, from his side of the bridge. 'There's some dirty weather knocking about. Go and look at the glass.'

When Jukes came out of the chart-room, the cast of his countenance had changed to thoughtfulness and concern. He caught hold of the bridge-rail and stared ahead.

The temperature in the engine-room had gone up to a hundred and seventeen degrees. Irritated voices were ascending through the skylight and through the fiddle of the stokehold in a harsh and resonant uproar, mingled with angry clangs and scrapes of metal, as if men with limbs of iron and throats of bronze had been quarrelling down there. The second engineer was failing foul of the stokers for letting the steam go down. He was a man with arms like a blacksmith, and generally feared; but that afternoon the stokers were answering him back recklessly, and slammed the furnace doors with the fury of despair. Then the noise ceased suddenly, and the second engineer appeared, emerging out of the stokehold streaked with grime and soaking wet like a chimney-sweep coming out of a well. As soon as his head was clear of the fiddle he began to scold Jukes for not trimming properly the stokehold ventilators; and in answer Jukes made with his hands deprecatory soothing signs meaning: 'No wind – can't be helped – you can see for yourself.' But the other wouldn't hear reason. His teeth flashed angrily in his dirty face ... All the Chinamen on deck appeared at their last gasp.

At its setting the sun had a diminished diameter and an expiring brown, rayless glow, as if millions of centuries elapsing since the morning had brought it near its end. A dense bank of cloud became visible to the northward; it had a sinister dark olive tint, and lay low and motionless upon the sea, resembling a solid obstacle in the path of the ship. She went floundering towards it like an exhausted creature driven to his death. The coppery twilight retired slowly, and the darkness brought out overhead a swarm of unsteady, big stars, that, as if blown upon, flickered exceedingly and seemed to hang very near the earth.

... The ship, after a pause of comparative steadiness, started upon a series of rolls, one worse than the other, and for a time Jukes, preserving his equilibrium, was too busy to open his mouth. As soon as the violent swinging had quieted down somewhat, he said: 'This is a bit too much of a good thing. Whether anything is coming or not I think she ought to be put head on to that swell. The old man is just gone in to lie down. Hang me if I don't speak to him.'

But when he opened the door of the chart-room he saw his captain reading a book. Captain MacWhirr was not lying down: he was standing up with one hand grasping the edge of the bookshelf and the other holding open before his face a thick volume. The lamp wriggled in the gimbals, the loosened books toppled from side to side on the shelf, the long barometer swung in jerky circles, the table altered its slant every moment. In the midst of all this stir and movement Captain MacWhirr, holding on, showed his eyes above the upper edge, and asked, 'What's the matter?'

'Swell getting worse, sir.'

'Noticed that in here,' muttered Captain MacWhirr. 'Anything wrong?'

He had been reading the chapter on the storms. When he had entered the chart-room, it was with no intention of taking the book down. Some influence in the air – the same influence, probably, that caused the steward to bring without orders the Captain's sea-boots and oilskin coat up to the chartroom – had as it were guided his hand to the shelf; and without taking the time to sit down he had waded with a conscious effort into the terminology of the subject. He lost himself amongst advancing semi-circles, left- and right-hand quadrants, the curves of the tracks, the probable bearing of the centre, the shifts of wind and the readings of barometer. He tried to bring all these things into a definite relation to himself; and ended by becoming contemptuously angry with such a lot of words and with so much advice, all head-work and supposition, without a glimmer of certitude.

HERODOTUS, from The History

Arion, they say, who was spending the greater part of his time at the court of Periander, was seized with a longing to sail to Italy and Sicily; but when he had made a great deal of money there, he wanted to come home to Corinth. So he set sail from Tarentum, and, as he trusted no people more than the Corinthians, he hired a boat of men of Corinth. But when they were out to sea, those Corinthians plotted to throw Arion overboard and take his money. When he understood what they would be at, he begged for his life at the sacrifice of the money. However, he could not prevail on them, and they, who were his ferrymen, bade him either kill himself – that he might have a grave when he was landed – or straightway jump into the sea. So, penned in helplessness, Arion besought them, since they were so determined, to stand by and watch him while he sang, standing with all his gear on him on the poop deck of the ship; he promised, once he had sung, to make away with himself. They for their part thought what a pleasure it would be for them to hear the greatest singer in the world, and so they retreated from the stern of the boat to amidships. He put on all his gear, took his lyre in his hand, and taking his stance on the poop went through the High Shrill Song, and, when it was finished, cast himself into the sea, just as he was, with all his gear. Away they sailed to Corinth; but, says the tale, a dolphin picked Arion up on his back and brought him back to Taenarum. He disembarked from the dolphin and went to Corinth (with all his gear) and, on his coming, told all that had happened to him. Periander – for he didn't believe him – held Arion under guard, suffering him to go nowhere else at all, and kept vigilant watch for his ferrymen. When they came, they were summoned to his presence and asked if they had any news of Arion. Yes, they said, he must be safe somewhere in Italy, since they had left him prospering in Tarentum. At that moment Arion appeared before them just as he was when he had leaped into the sea; whereupon they, in their utter confusion, were unable to deny what was brought home to them. This is what the Corinthians and

Lesbians say, and there is at Taenerum a small dedicatory offering to Arion, made of bronze and figuring a man riding upon a dolphin.

The sicknesses are now gone, vanished, expelled, and sailed away

We rarely took lessons outside of school, and there was little organized sport. All questions as to precedence or selection were decided by playing *Junk an' a Po*, a game of scissors, stone, and rock; three out of five rounds were sufficient to settle almost anything. My Japanese friends went to Japan School in the late afternoon so as not to forget their heritage, although I never heard any of them speak Japanese, nor did they seem overly interested in their heritage. If a Japanese girl were caught with a boy who was not Japanese, however, she would disappear overnight – only years later did we realize that she'd been whisked to Japan for safekeeping. (Kidnapping was also employed to dispose of unmarried girls who became pregnant, some of whom only returned to the Islands as grown women, having long given up their illegitimate children for adoption.) An elderly, rather elegant French woman, always dressed in damp pastel chiffon and a large flowered hat, was my French tutor. She gave genteel but nonetheless intriguing hints that her position in life previous to that of tutor to restless children in the tropics had been somewhat more distinguished, if not downright glamorous. It was not until years later, sitting in a dark movie theater, that I recognized Madame as lady's maid to Luise Rainer in *The Great Ziegfeld.* One very hot summer, I was inexplicably compelled by my mother to take sewing lessons from a Japanese seamstress in downtown Honolulu, an ambitious although slightly loony project. No thought was given as to just how I was to reach Mrs. Kimura's rooms with the result that a two-hour bus ride, each way, was necessary. I sewed a brown-and-white plaid sleeveless dress made of shagbark (does such a material still exist?) with a brown cummerbund that I wore to shreds even though the hem had been finished with masking tape.

I was not given much spending money (I remember saving to buy a small brown paper sack of raisins) and indeed I did not need it. My mother was not only generous when necessary, but could effortlessly enter the imagination of a child, despite the Best and Co. brown shoes. When I was ten, I determined the need for a professional portrait and took myself to the studio of a Japanese photographer that I'd often passed on my bus ride home. He did not speak English – his business was mail-order bride portraits, I soon realized – but he did not question my somewhat odd request, which I demonstrated with hand signs and a few words of pidgin English. Nor did my mother question it when I asked her for the exorbitant sum of money he demanded for rather too many girlish poses (eighteen), nine of them with my chin resting lightly in my palm.

We were rarely taken to a restaurant, and then only on a Sunday night for Chinese food. There was little television – *Captain Honolulu*, a cartoon show, was much admired – and only on the weekend. Sunday evening at six o'clock, servants and children watched television together, both contingents intensely loyal to a local program called *Televi Digest* in which people (not *haoles*) did laborious magic tricks or sang and danced for prizes. Our transistor radios were much valued. Listening to the adults' long-playing records, we knew every word of the songs in *Carousel*, *Ahmal and the Night Visitors*, and *Pal Joey*. We did not have much use of the telephone. Later, when we might have availed ourselves of it, the placement of the children's telephone in the kitchen did not encourage private conversation, which may have been the intention.

I often went to the Outrigger Canoe Club in Waikiki after school and on the weekend. When I was nine, I was taught to ride a surfboard by the beach-boy Rabbit Kekai (who still surfs; his picture was in the *New York Times* recently in an article about elderly surfers) on a long wooden board. Ankle bands that attach by plastic cord to the board had not been invented. Neither Rabbit not myself found it unseemly or even uncomfortable to assume our position – I would lie on my stomach facing the front of the board with my legs pleasantly spread so that he could slide on behind me. He also lay on his stomach, between my legs, his chin resting on my bottom. We both used our arms to paddle out to the break at Queen's Surf.

My mother died the summer that I was twelve years old, and my father, somewhat impulsively, gave me two pieces of her jewelry – a necklace of fat pink pearls and a large emerald ring, with the injunction that I was too young to wear them. The pearls held no interest for me then, but the ring was chimerical. It was heavy on my hand and noticeably unsuitable for a girl. Despite my father's request and without attracting his notice, I wore it.

One afternoon when I had progressed suffi-ciently in my surfing lessons to go to the reef alone, I entrusted the ring, sealed in a little brown envelope, to one of the men sitting in the beachboys' shack. When I returned, exhilarated and proud, dragging the awkward board up the beach to collect my ring, no one could recall having seen a ring. It must be in the sea, they said (rendered in Pidgin English, 'Da ocean gone cockaroach 'em'). The feeling of confusion and, more fatal to me, betrayal was so strong that I could not speak. Some weeks later, inexplicably, my father granted me permission to wear the ring to dinner. I was too ashamed to admit that it had been stolen and by people whom I believed to be my friends, so I told him that I had lost it. He looked at me for some time, and then said, 'I will never give you another piece of jewelry,' and he didn't.

SIR JAMES GEORGE FRAZER, *from* The Golden Bough

'The Occasional Expulsion of Evils in a Material Vehicle'

The vehicle which conveys away the demon may be of various kinds. A common one is a little ship or boat. Thus, in the southern district of the island of Ceram, when a whole village suffers from sickness, a small ship is made and filled with rice, tobacco, eggs, and so forth, which have been contributed by all the people. A little sail is hoisted on the ship. When all is ready, a man calls out in a very loud voice, 'O all ye sicknesses, ye smallpoxes, agues, measles, etc., who have visited us so long and wasted us so sorely, but who now cease to plague us, we have made ready this ship for you, and we have furnished you with provender sufficient for the voyage. Ye shall have no lack of food nor of betel-leaves nor of areca nuts nor of tobacco. Depart, and sail away from us directly; never come near us again; but go to a land which is far from here. Let all the tides and winds waft you speedily thither, and so convey you thither that for the time to come we may live sound and well, and that we may never see the sun rise on you again.' Then ten or twelve men carry the vessel to the shore, and let it drift away with the land-breeze, feeling convinced that they are free from sickness for ever or at least till the next time. If sickness attacks them again, they are sure it is not the same sickness, but a different one, which in due time they dismiss in the same manner. When the demon-laden bark is lost to sight the bearers return to the village, whereupon a man cries out, 'The sicknesses are now gone, vanished, expelled, and sailed away.'

FORD MADOX FORD, *from* Joseph Conrad

At any rate Conrad, by all accounts, was a very admirable officer. Yet he hated the sea ... Over and over again he related how overwhelming, with his small stature, he found negotiations with heavy spars, stubborn cordage and black weather. He used to say, half raising his arms, 'Look at me ... How was I made for such imbecilities? Besides, my nerves were for ever on the racket ...' And he would recount how, when he had been running up the Channel on a moonlight night, suddenly, right under the foot of the *Torrens*, there had appeared the ghostly sails of a small vessel. It was, he used to say, something supernatural, something of the sort that was always happening at sea. He said it wasn't so much that his heart was in

his mouth for the seconds it took that vessel to clear;
it remained in his mouth for months after.

THOMAS MANN, *from* Death in Venice

At times – of a forenoon perhaps, as he lay in the
shadow of his awning, gazing out dreamily over the
blue of the southern sea, or in the mildness of the
night, beneath the wide starry sky, ensconced among
the cushions of the gondola that bore him Lido-wards
after an evening on the Piazza, while the gay lights
faded and the melting music of the serenades died
away on his ear – he would think of his mountain
home, the theatre of his summer labours. There
clouds hung low and tailed through the garden,
violent storms extinguished the lights of the house at
night, and the ravens he fed swung in the tops of the
fir trees. And he would feel transported to Elysium,
to the ends of the earth, to a spot most carefree for
the sons of men, where no snow is, and no winter, no

73

storms or downpours of rain; where Oceanus send a mild and cooling breath, and days flow on in blissful idleness, without effort or struggle, entirely dedicated to the sun and the feasts of the sun ...

He would see him coming up, on the left, along the margin of the sea; or from behind, between the cabins; or, with a start of joyful surprise, would discover that he himself was late, and Tadzio already down, in the blue and white bathing-suit that was now his only wear on the beach; there and engrossed in his usual activities in the sand, beneath the sun. It was a sweetly idle, trifling, fitful life, of play and rest, of strolling, wading, digging, fishing, swimming, lying on the sand. Often the women sitting on the platform would call out to him in their high voices: 'Tadziu! Tadziu!' and he would come running and waving his arms, eager to tell them what he had found, what caught – shells, seahorses, jelly-fish, and sidewards-running crabs. Aschenbach understood not a word he said; it might be the sheerest commonplace, in his ear it became mingled harmonies. Thus the lad's foreign birth raised his speech to music; a wanton sun showered splendour on him, and the noble distances of the sea formed the background which set off his figure.

WALT WHITMAN, from Leaves of Grass

'Out of the Rolling Ocean the Crowd'

Out of the rolling ocean the crowd came a
    drop gently to me,
Whispering *I love you, before long I die,*
I have travel'd a long way merely to look on you
    to touch you,
For I could not die till I once look'd on you,
For I fear'd I might afterward lose you,
Now we have met, we have look'd, we are safe,
Return in peace to the ocean my love,
I too am part of that ocean my love, we are
    not so much separated,
Behold the great rondure, the cohesion of
    all, how perfect!

But as for me, for you, the irresistible sea is
   to separate us,
As for an hour carrying us diverse, yet
   cannot carry us diverse forever;
Be not impatient – a little pace – know you
   I salute the air, the ocean and the land,
Every day at sundown for your dear sake
   my love.

VIRGINIA WOOLF, from To the Lighthouse

All the way down to the beach they had lagged behind together, though he bade them 'Walk up, walk up,' without speaking. Their heads were bent down, their heads were pressed down by some remorseless gale. Speak to him they could not. They must come; they must follow. They must walk behind him carrying brown paper parcels. But they vowed, in silence, as they walked, to stand by each other and carry out the great compact – to resist tyranny to the death. So there they would sit, one at one end of the boat, one at the other, in silence. They would say nothing, only look at him now and then where he sat with his legs twisted, frowning and fidgeting, and pishing and pshawing and muttering things to himself, and waiting impatiently for a breeze. And they hoped it would be calm. They hoped he would be thwarted. They hoped the whole expedition would fail, and they would have to put back, with their parcels, to the beach.

But now, when Macalister's boy had rowed a little way out, the sails slowly swung round, the boat quickened itself, flattened itself, and shot off. Instantly, as if some great strain had been relieved, Mr Ramsay uncurled his legs, took out his tobacco pouch, handed it with a little grunt to Macalister, and felt, they knew, for all they suffered, perfectly content. Now they would sail on for hours like this, and Mr Ramsay would ask old Macalister a question – about the great storm last winter probably – and old Macalister would answer it, and they would puff their pipes together, and Macalister would take a tarry rope in his fingers, tying or untying some knot, and the boy would fish, and never say a word to any one. James would be forced to keep his eye all the time on the sail. For if he forgot, then the sail puckered, and shivered, and the boat slackened, and Mr Ramsay would say sharply: 'Look out! Look out!' and old Macalister would turn slowly on his seat. So they heard Mr Ramsay asking some question about the great storm at Christmas. 'She comes driving round the point,' old Macalister said, describing the great storm at Christmas, when ten ships had been driven into the bay for shelter, and he had seen 'one there, one there, one there' (he pointed slowly round the bay. Mr Ramsay followed him, turning his head). He had seen three men clinging to the mast. Then she was gone. 'And at last we shoved her off,' he went on (but in their anger and their silence they only caught a word here and there, sitting at opposite ends of the boat, united by their compact to fight tyranny to the death). At last they had shoved her off, they had launched the lifeboat, and they had got her out past the point – Macalister told the story;

and though they only caught a word here and there, they were conscious all the time of their father – how he leant forward, how he brought his voice into tune with Macalister's voice; how, puffing at his pipe, and looking there and there where Macalister pointed, he relished the thought of the storm and the dark night and the fishermen striving there. He liked that men should labour and sweat on the windy beach at night, pitting muscle and brain against the waves and the wind; he liked men to work like that, and women to keep house, and sit beside sleeping children indoors, while men were drowned, out there in a storm ...

... Yes, the breeze was freshening. The boat was leaning, the water was sliced sharply and fell away in green cascades, in bubbles, in cataracts. Cam looked down into the foam, into the sea with all its treasure in it, and its speed hypnotized her, and the time between her and James sagged a little. It slackened a little. She began to think, How fast it goes. Where are we going? and the movement hypnotized her, while James, with his eye fixed on the sail and on the horizon, steered grimly. But he began to think as he steered that he might escape; he might be quit of it all. They might land somewhere; and be free then. Both of them, looking at each other for a moment, had a sense of escape and exaltation, what with the speed and the change. But the breeze bred in Mr Ramsay too the same excitement, and, as old Macalister turned to fling his line overboard, he cried aloud: 'We are perished,' and then again, 'each alone.' And then with his usual spasm of repentance or shyness, pulled himself up, and waved his hand toward the shore.

J. W. GOETHE, from Goethe's Travels in Italy (1786–1788)

19 October, from Ferrara to Rome

I cannot help reminding my friends of a dream which I had about a year ago, and which appeared to me to be highly significant. I dreamt forsooth, that I had been sailing about in a little boat and had landed on a fertile and richly cultivated island, of which I had a consciousness that it bred the most beautiful pheasants in the world. I bargained, I thought, with the people of the island for some of these birds, and they killed and brought them to me in great numbers. They were pheasants indeed, but as in dreams all things are generally changed and modified, they seemed to have long, richly coloured tails, like the loveliest birds of Paradise, and with eyes like those of the peacock. Bringing them to me by scores, they arranged them in the boat so skilfully with the heads inwards, the long variegated feathers of the tail hanging outwards, as to form in the bright sunshine the most glorious pile conceivable, and so large as scarcely to leave room enough in the bow and the stern for the rower and the steersman. As with this load the boat made its way through the tranquil waters, I named to myself the friends among whom I should like to distribute those variegated treasures. At last, arriving in a spacious harbour, I was almost lost among great and many masted vessels, as I mounted deck after deck in order

to discover a place where I might safely run my little
boat ashore.

HENRY JAMES, *from*
The Portrait of a Lady

There was an indefinable beauty about him – in his
situation, in his mind, in his face. She had felt at the
same time that he was helpless and ineffectual, but
the feeling had taken the form of a tenderness which
was the very flower of respect. He was like a sceptical
voyager, strolling on the beach while he waited for
the tide, looking seaward yet not putting to sea. It
was in all this that she found her occasion, She would
launch his boat for him; she would be his providence;
it would be a good thing to love him.

IV

Asleep in the arms of the slow-swinging sea

In our ravishing little world, there were no visible Jews or visible homosexuals of either sex. There were African-Americans in the military, but we rarely saw them. The military families were considered a bit lower-class. The girls were quite startling. They were flirtatious, accustomed to being around thousands of men conveniently organized into ranks. They were almost always blond and they wore Dr. Scholl's sandals to school. Raised in a hierarchy that was blatant, they were, unlike us, unembarrassed by ambition. They were also thought to be a little fast, but that wasn't why they were never quite accepted. It was island snobbery. The disdain of the clerisy.

There was a fairly unconscious racism all around us, although not toward Hawaiians, perhaps because they were not competitive. We thought them above approach, at any rate. We were unaware that the racism had long been institutionalized, but our parents and teachers knew, and sanctioned the restrictions and bylaws that kept non-*haole*s not only from private clubs, but from certain neighborhoods. These restrictions are ended now (sometimes by court decision), but in 1958 they were unquestioned by either side.

Later, I was astonished to learn that only *haole*s were allowed to live in the most desirable neighborhoods – Diamond Head and Kahala, for example – especially as there were three generations of Hawaiian fishermen, quite a number of children and dogs, and an irritable but dignified *tutu* (grandmother) in black *holoku*, *ilima* lei, and trim straw hat who lived in a compound on the beach at the bottom of our garden in Kahala. 'Squatters,' my uncle explained when asked about this mysterious and jolly family. I spent quite a bit of time with them. Years later, I went to see the Worthingtons (descendants of an English sea captain? You see the dangers of myth), but they had disappeared. My uncle does not remember them.

Despite (or because of) the unacknowledged divisions of class and race, there was no ostentation of wealth or power. Women did not wear jewels (or even dresses); no one drove an expensive car, nor indulged in visibly fancy vice. A few people were worldly enough to collect very good Asian art, which could be had for a song, especially after the war and the fall of the Kuomintang government in China. If a holiday trip were made, it was not to Paris, but to Melbourne or Denver. Older women were addressed by their first name, preceded by Miss or, less formally, Auntie. A friend of mine, now in her eighties, is known as Auntie Sis. Her own sisters were Auntie Red and Auntie Old Lady (her name even as a girl). They are the descendants of a young sailor shipwrecked in the Islands in the 19th century and found asleep on the beach, naked, by one of the king's daughters who at once desired to marry him – a myth reminiscent of Odysseus and Nausicaa. Auntie Sis, as do those women of her age and class who are still alive, speaks with an antiquated aristocratic accent, somewhat English, passed down from the Yankee missionaries and Scots cabin boys who were her ancestors. 'Do you remembah when we use to swim the hosses?' she will ask. 'You were a little gel then.'

Although the Hawaiians were admired and even idealized, there was little interest in Hawaiian culture. We learned hula, but it was always a *hapa-haole* hula, like 'My Little Grass Shack' or 'Lovely Hula Hands'. A Hawaiian woman, Miss Alice, who sometimes looked after us when our father and step-mother were away, at my insistence taught me over the years the Hawaiian words of the old songs (oddly, I did not then know their meaning, having learned them by rote). She told me angrily (I could not tell: Was she angry with the Hawaiians or with me?) that the people had turned away from everything; the beautiful as well as the practical. Her great-grand-father had been interpreter of omens for a chief of O'ahu, but her children could not speak Hawaiian. She was perversely pleased that many of the old secrets had been lost – the location of the *'ape'ape* herb found only in the damp mountain gullies of east Maui or the recipe for the love potion made from the last remaining stalks of red sugarcane. She said that there were very few people left who could speak with any certainty about the past. 'The old meles and the old hen-tales are nearly forgotten, as are the old hulas,' wrote Mrs. Gerould. 'A few aged men and women can still sing and dance in traditional fashion ... but there is no one to whom they can pass on the words of the songs or the motions of the dance. The new songs are different – lyrical at best, never epic; and the new dances might perhaps delight a cabaret, if any cabaret could conceivably be allowed to present them ... The old hulas were different; were stately and, I dare say, a little tiresome, with their monotonous swaying and arm gestures repeated a thousand times. Only a very old person now can dance in the earlier fashion; you could easily count up the Hawaiians who know the meles; and there is just one man, I believe, left on Oahu (if indeed he is still living) who can play the nose-flute as it should be played, to the excruciation of every nerve in a Caucasian body.'

A few years ago, a friend was walking on the beach at her family's house in Malaekahana when she chanced to see a turtle, the size and shape of a quarter, staggering across the sand to the sea. The turtle, after many cumbersome attempts, at last tumbled into the surf where, to my friend's dismay, it began to drown. She waded into the water to save it. It was not easy to see it in the white water, but, miraculously, she found it. The turtle was not strong enough to keep afloat, so she ferried it past the breaking surf to calmer water, where it sank to the bottom. She is a good swimmer, like all island girls, and with two or three dives, she found it just as it was disappearing into deep water. She carried it ashore in the palm of her hand and filled a child's wading pool with warm seawater. She bought raw bait, and chopped it into minuscule pieces to feed the turtle. After a few hours, when it grew apparent that the turtle was dying, she called the Oceanographic Institute near Makapu'u to inquire if she should alter the turtle's diet or the temperature of the water. She was astonished to learn upon describing the turtle – although not as astonished as the oceanographer – that she had found a species last seen sixty years ago, so rare as to be thought extinct.

Her picture with the turtle balanced on the tip of her finger was on the front page of the *Honolulu Advertiser* and she was given a lifetime pass to the institute, which promptly confiscated the turtle.

By the end of the 1960s, we seldom went to Waikiki – once suburban shopping malls were built and the Outrigger Canoe Club moved to its present place near Diamond Head, there was no reason to go there. Only tourists and hustlers went to Waikiki. Alternative roads were built so that we did not even have to drive through Waikiki. We seldom went downtown except for trips to the dentist or doctor with an office in the old Alexander Young Hotel Building (the coffee shop famous for coconut-cream pie, packed in a pale pink box to take home).

Not everyone felt the same curiosity about Hawai'i and its culture and history that possessed me; my parents and their friends preferred swimming in a chlorinated pool to the ocean and traveled to San Francisco sooner than to Hilo. The study of Hawaiian culture, and the awareness of a specific and important history was to come in the 1980s, to the point that many activists today demand the sovereignty of a Hawaiian nation. Many of my friends now learn to speak Hawaiian, to dance hula with a strict *kumu hula* (teacher), to make Hawaiian quilts (in old times, said Miss Alice, the pattern came to a woman in a dream), to cook *luau*, to build outrigger canoes by hand. It is fashionable for *haole* men to belong to local clubs that race ocean canoes. In the 1950s, however, Hawaiiana was not yet a business. Stores did not possess large sections given to calendars of Filipino beach-boys, and cookbooks with imaginative breadfruit recipes, and anthologies of local murders – the result of an increase in tourism as well as the growing sense of a Hawaiian identity. The happy result, however, even if it is tinged with post-modernist interpretation or New Age philosophy (the practice of the latter largely confined to Maui, which is why I no longer go there), is the new scholarship and the publication of many good books. Mu'umu'us are no longer worn, however. Some of the women who have lunch at the Outrigger Canoe Club wear Chanel suits, high heels, jewelry, and stockings – I must admit that in my own provincial way I am very shocked by the stockings. In India, I have noticed, many women have forsaken the sari for the *salwar kameez*, but that is about ease of movement and comfort, the opposite of the mu'umu'u, which, in the end, turned out to be extremely practical as well as comfortable. The irony, of course, is that the disappearance of everything is just what has allowed us to see it.

RUDYARD KIPLING, *from* Rudyard Kipling's Verse

'Seal Lullaby'

Oh Hush thee, my baby,
the night is behind us,
And black are the waters
that sparkled so green.
The moon, o'er the combers,
looks downward to find us
At rest in the hollows that rustle between.

Where billow meets billow,
there soft be thy pillow;
Ah! Weary wee flippering,
curl at thy ease!
The storm shall not wake thee,
nor shark overtake thee,
Asleep in the arms
of the slow-swinging seas.

HENRY WILLIAMSON, from
Tarka the Otter

Six hours later Tarka ran up Wild Pear Beach and his thin, hard cries pierced the slop and wash of waves on the loose, worn, shaley strand. He followed the trail over the weeds to the otters' sleeping place under a rock, and down again to the sea. In a pool off Briery Cave he scented otter again, for at the bottom of the pool lay a wicker pot, holding something that turned slowly as the ribbons of the thongweed lifted and dropped in the water. The red feelers of a dark blue lobster were thrust through the wickerwork; it was gorged, and trying to get away from the otter cub it had been eating. The cub had found no way out of the cage it had entered at high tide, intending to eat the lobster.

Hu-ee-ic! Tarka did not know the dead. Nothing answered, and he swam away, among green phosphoric specks that glinted at every wave-lop.

Autumn's little summer, when day and night were equal, and only the woodlark sang his wistful falling song over the bracken, was ruined by the gales that tore wave and leaf, and broke the sea into roar and spray, and hung white ropes over the rocks. Fog hid cliff-tops and stars as Tarka travelled westwards. One night, as he was drinking fresh water from a pool below a cascade, he was startled by immense whooping bellows that bounded from the walls of mist and rebounded afar, to return in duller echoes as though phantom hounds were baying in the darkness. Tarka slipped into a pool and hid under lifting seaweed; but the sounds were regular and harmless, and afterwards he did not heed them. On a rock below the white-walled tower of Bull Point lighthouse, whose twin sirens were sending a warning to sailors far out beyond the dreadful rocks, Tarka found again the trail of White-tip, and whistled with joy.

Travelling under the screes, where rusted plates of wrecked ships lay in pools, he came to the end of the land. Day was beginning. The tide, moving north-wards across Morte Bay from Bag Leap, was ripped and whitened by rocks which stood out of the hollows of the grey sea. One rock was tall about the reef – the Morte Stone – and on the top pinnacle stood a big black bird, with the tails of fish sticking out of its gullet. Its dripping wings were held out to ease its tight crop. The bird was Phalacrocorax Carbo, called the Isle-of-Wight Parson by fishermen, and it sat uneasily on the Morte Stone during most of the hours of daylight, swaying with a load of fishes.

Tired and buffeted by the long Atlantic rollers, Tarka turned back under the Morte Stone, and swam to land. He climbed a slope strewn with broken thrift roots and grey shards of rock, to a path set on its seaward verge by a fence of iron posts and cables. Salt winds had gnawed the iron to rusty splinters. The heather above the path was tougher that the iron, but its sprigs were barer than its own roots.

Over the crest of the Morte heather grew in low bushes, out of the wind's way. There were green places where, among grass cropped by sheep, grew mushrooms mottled like owls' plumage. The sky above the crest was reddening, and he found a sleeping place under a broken cromlech, the burial place of an ancient man, whose bones were grass and heather and dust in the sun.

ALFRED, LORD TENNYSON, from Poems

'The Mermaid'

I
Who would be
A mermaid fair, Singing alone,
Combing her hair

Under the sea,
In a golden curl
With a comb of pearl
On a throne?

II

I would be a mermaid fair;
I would sing to myself the whole of the
    day;
With a comb of pearl I would comb my
    hair;
And still as I comb'd I would sing and say,
'Who is it loves me? Who loves not me?'
I would comb my hair till my ringlets
    would fall
Low adown, low adown,
From under my starry sea-bud crown
Low adown and around,
And I should look like a fountain of gold
Springing alone
With a shrill inner sound
Over the throne

in the midst of the hall;
Till that great sea-snake under the sea
From his coiled sleeps in the central deeps
Would slowly trail himself sevenfold
Round the hall where I sate, and look in at
    the gate
With his large calm eyes for the love of me.
    And all the mermen under the sea
Would feel their immortality
Die in their hearts for the love of me.

III
But at night I would wander away, away,
I would fling on each side my low-flowing
    locks,
And lightly vault from the throne and play
With the mermen in and out of the rocks;
We would run to and fro, and hide and
    seek,
On the broad sea-wolds in the crimson
    shells,
Whose silvery spikes are nighest the sea,

But if any came near I would call and shriek,
And adown the steep like a wave I would leap
From the diamond-ledges that jut from the
    dells;
For I would not be kiss'd by all who would list
Of the bold merry mermen under the sea.
They would sue me, and woo me, and
    flatter me,
In the purple twilights under the sea;
But the king of them all would carry me,
Woo me, and win me, and marry me,
In the branching jaspers under the sea.
Then all the dry-pied things that be
In the hueless mosses under the sea
Would curl round my silver feet silently,
All looking up for the love of me.
And if I should carol aloud, from aloft
All things that are forked, and homed, and
    soft
Would lean out from the hollow sphere of
    the sea,
All looking down for the love of me.

THOR HEYERDAHL, *from*
The Kon-Tiki Expedition

Sometimes, too, we went out in the rubber boat to look at ourselves by night. Coal-black seas towered up on all sides, and a glittering myriad of tropical stars drew a faint reflection from plankton in the water. The world was simple – stars in the darkness. Whether it was 1947 B.C. or A.D. suddenly became of no significance. We lived, and that we felt with alert intensity. We realized that life had been full for men before the technical age also – in fact, fuller and richer in many ways than the life of modern man. Time and evolution somehow ceased to exist; all that was real and that mattered were the same today as they had always been and would always be. We were swallowed up in the absolute common measure of history – endless unbroken darkness under a swarm of stars.

Before us in the night the *Kon-Tiki* rose out of the seas to sink down again behind black masses of water that towered between her and us. In the moonlight there was a fantastic atmosphere about the raft. Stout, shining wooden logs fringed with seaweed, the square pitch-black outline of a Viking sail, a bristly bamboo hut with the yellow light of a paraffin lamp aft – the whole suggested a picture from a fairytale rather than an actual reality. Now and then the raft disappeared completely behind the black seas; then she rose again and stood out sharp in silhouette against the stars, while glittering water poured from the logs.

When we saw the atmosphere about the solitary raft, we could well see in our mind's eye the whole flotilla of such vessels, spread in fan formation beyond the horizon to increase the chances of finding land, when the first men made their way across this sea. The Inca Tupac Yupanqui, who had brought under his rule both Peru and Ecuador, sailed across the sea with an armada of many thousand men on balsa rafts, just before the Spaniards came, to search for islands which rumor had told of out in the Pacific. He found two islands, which some think were the Galapagos, and after eight months' absence he and his numerous paddlers succeeded in toiling their way back to Ecuador.

~

... On the night before July 30 there was a new and strange atmosphere about the *Kon-Tiki*. Perhaps it was the deafening clamor from all the sea birds over us which showed that something fresh was brewing. The screaming of birds with many voices sounded hectic and earthly after the dead creaking of lifeless ropes, which was all we had heard above the noise of the sea in the three months we had behind us. And the moon seemed larger and rounder than ever as it sailed over the lookout at the masthead. In our fancy it reflected palm tops and warm-blooded romance; it did not shine with such a yellow light over the cold fishes out at sea.

... Land! An island! We devoured it greedily with our eyes and woke the others, who tumbled out drowsily and stared in all directions as if they thought our bow was about to run on to a beach. Screaming sea birds formed a bridge across the sky in the direction of the distant island, which stood out sharper against the horizon as the red background widened and turned gold with the approach of the sun and the full daylight.

Our first thought was that the island did not lie where it should. As the island could not have drifted, the raft must have been caught up in a northward current in the course of the night. We had only to cast one glance over the sea to perceive at once, from the direction of the waves, that we had lost our chance in the darkness. Where we now lay, the wind no longer allowed us to press the raft on a course toward the island. The region round the Tuamotu Archipelago was fill of strong, local ocean currents which twisted in all directions as they ran up against land; many of them varied in direction as they met powerful tidal currents flowing in and out over reefs and lagoons.

We laid the steering oar over, but we knew quite well that it was useless …

… No extravagant outbursts were to be heard on board. After the sail had been trimmed and the oar laid over, we all formed a silent group at the masthead or stood on deck staring toward the land which had suddenly cropped up out in the middle of the endless, all-dominating sea. At last we had a visible proof that we had really been moving in all these months; we had not just been lying tumbling about in the center of the same eternal circular horizon. To us it seemed as if the island were mobile and had suddenly entered the circle of blue and empty sea in the center of which we had our permanent abode; as if the island were drifting slowly across our own domain, heading for the eastern horizon. We were all filled with a warm, quiet satisfaction at having actually reached Polynesia, mingled with a faint momentary disappointment at having to submit helplessly to seeing the island lie there like a mirage while we continued our eternal drift across the sea westward.

D. H. LAWRENCE, from
The Complete Poems

'Whales Weep Not!'

They say the sea is cold, but the sea
    contains the hottest blood of all, and the
    wildest, the most urgent.
All the whales in the wider deeps, hot are
    they, as they urge on and on and dive
    beneath the icebergs.
The right whales, the sperm-whales, the
    hammer-heads, the killers
there they blow, there they blow, hot wild
    white breath out of the sea!

And they rock, and they rock through the
    sensual ageless ages
on the depths of the seven seas,
and through the salt they reel with drunk
    delight
and in the tropics tremble they with love

and roll with massive, strong desire, like gods.
Then the great bull lies up against his
    bride
in the blue deep bed of the sea,
as mountain pressing on mountain, in the
    zest of life
and out of the inward roaring of the inner
    red ocean of whale-blood
the long tip reaches strong, intense, like
    the maelstrom-tip, and comes to rest
in the clasp and the soft, wild clutch of a
    she-whale's fathomless body.

And over the bridge of the whale's strong
    phallus, linking the wonder of whales
the burning archangels under the sea keep
    passing, back and forth,
keep passing, archangels of bliss
from him to her, from her to him, great
    Cherubim
that wait on whales in mid-ocean,
    suspended in the waves of

the
sea
great heaven of whales in the waters, old
   hierarchies.

And enormous mother whales lie dreaming
   suckling their whale-tender young
and dreaming with strange whale eyes wide
   open in the waters
of
the beginning and the end.
And bull-whales gather their women and
   whale-calves in a ring
when danger threatens, on the surface of
   the ceaseless flood
and range themselves like great fierce
   Seraphim facing the threat
encircling their huddled monsters of love.
And all this happens in the sea, in the salt
   where God is also love, but without words:
and Aphrodite is the wife of whales most
   happy, happy she!

And Venus among the fishes slaps and is a
    sea-dolphin
she is the gay, delighted porpoise sporting
    with love and the
sea
she is the female tunny-fish, round and
    happy among the males
and dense with happy blood, dark rainbow
    bliss in the sea.

PLINY, from Letters

TO CANINIUS RUFUS. I have met with a story, which, though true, has all the air of fable, and would afford a very proper subject for your lively, elevated, and truly poetical genius. It was related to me the other day at table, where the conversation happened to turn upon various kinds of miraculous events. The person who gave the account, was a man of unsuspected veracity – but what has a poet to do with truth? However, you might venture to rely upon his testimony, even though you had the character of a faithful historian to support.

There is in Africa a town called Hippo, situated not far from the sea-coast: it stands upon a navigable lake, from whence an estuary is discharged after the manner of a river, which ebbs and flows with the sea. Persons of all ages divert themselves here with fishing, sailing or swimming; especially boys, whom love of play and idleness bring hither. The contest among them is, who shall have the glory of swimming farthest; and he that leaves the shore and his companions at the greatest distance, gains the victory. It happened in one of these trials of skill, that a certain boy, more bold than the rest, launched out towards the opposite shore. He was met by a dolphin, who sometimes swam before him, and sometimes behind him, then played round him, and at last took him on his back, then let him down, and afterwards took him up again: and thus carried the poor frightened boy out into the deepest part; when immediately he turns back again to the shore, and lands him among his companions.

The fame of this remarkable accident spread through the town, and crowds of people flocked round the boy (whom they viewed as a kind of prodigy) to ask him questions, hear his story and repeat it.

The next day the shore was lined with multitudes of spectators all attentively observing the ocean, and (what is indeed almost itself an ocean) the lake. In the meanwhile the boys swam as usual, and among the rest, the youth I am speaking of went into the lake, but with more caution than before. The dolphin punctually appeared again and came to the boy, who together with his companions swam away with the utmost precipitation. The dolphin, as it were, to invite and recall them, bounded and dived up and down, winding about in a thousand different circles. This he practised for several days together, till the people (accustomed from their infancy to the sea) began to be ashamed of their timidity. They ventured therefore to advance nearer, playing with him and calling him to them, while he, in return, suffered himself to be touched and stroked. Use rendered them more courageous: the boy, in particular, who first made the experiment, swam by the side of him, and leaping upon his back, was carried to and fro in that manner: he fancies the dolphin knows and is fond of him, and he returns its fondness. There seemed now, indeed, to be no fear on either side, the confidence of the one and the tameness of the other mutually increasing; the rest of the boys in the meanwhile swimming on either hand, encouraging and cautioning their companion. It is very remarkable, that this dolphin was followed by a second, which seemed only as a spectator and attendant on the former; for he did not at all submit to the same familiarities as the first, but only conducted him backwards and forwards, as the boys did their comrade.

But what is incredible, yet no less true than the rest, this dolphin who thus played with the boys and carried them on his back, would come upon the shore, dry himself in the sand, and as soon as he grew warm, roll back into the sea. 'Tis known that Octavius Avitus, deputy governor of the province, from an absurd piece of superstition, poured some precious ointment over him as he lay on the shore, the novelty and smell of which made him retire into the ocean, and it was not till after several days that he was seen again, when he appeared dull and languid; however, he recovered his strength and continued his usual wanton tricks. All the magistrates round the country flocked hither to view this sight, the entertainment of whom upon their arrival, and during their stay, was an additional expense, which the slender finances of this little community could ill afford; besides, the quiet and retirement of the place was utterly destroyed. It was thought proper therefore to remove the occasion of this concourse, by privately killing the poor dolphin.

And now, with what flow of tenderness will you describe this sad catastrophe! and how will your genius adorn and heighten this moving story! Though, indeed, it does not require any fictitious embellishments; it will be sufficient to place the real circumstances in their full light.

ANONYMOUS, *from* The New Oxford Book of Irish Verse

Amerigin's Songs

III

Fish-teeming sea
abounding land
a flood of fish
fish under wave
like flights of birds
in the hard ocean.
A bright torrent
salmon in hundreds
plump creatures
harbour song:
A flood of fish
fish-teeming sea.

V

Say – Sea – Take me!

Once, swimming in front of the Royal Hawaiian Hotel in Waikiki when I was seven years old, I was lifted by a little wave and could no longer touch the bottom. I was, for a moment, drowning. As promised, my life passed before my eyes. The surge of high water gently withdrew and I was earthbound once again. At lunch, I made the adults laugh, which embarrassed me, when I admitted in disappointment that the events of my life had flitted past very quickly as I had not lived long enough to render the experience very interesting.

For some time, before moving farther from town to a country place on the ocean with wild and violent seas, we lived in a neighborhood half an hour from downtown Honolulu called Kahala. It was, and still

is, a fashionable and expensive place, reached by way of
the coast road from Diamond Head, or inland through
the then-primarily Japanese town of Kaimuki. I was
perplexed as a child that the most prestigious stretch
of land in the islands possessed the most unpleasant
beach. The water had a flat, opaque surface, grey in
color, with little movement, stretching placidly to a
low reef a half mile from shore indicated only by a
thin line of white – the sea breaking over the coral
– seemingly, in an optical illusion, only inches from
the horizon. In low tide, it was possible to walk to
the reef, but no one ever did. The bottom of clayish,
thick mud immediately enveloped your feet, the mud
seeping quite pleasurably between your toes. Chunks
of loose coral and rocks and broken glass and tin cans
littered the bottom. There was a sulfurous stench
at low tide because of the desiccation of the endless
organisms thriving in the mud. The beach was not
really good for anything but walking. A mile away,
Henry J. Kaiser had employed two enormous dredges
to dig a swimming hole in front of his house, and
sometimes we walked to Hunakai, as it was called,

to swim in the little hole cut from the shelf of coral and clay.

The Fullers, of the paint and brush company, lived next door to us in Kahala. It was at lunch with the Fuller children that I first saw an artichoke; the Fullers had lately moved to Honolulu from San Francisco. There was a serious but kind mother, and a boyishly handsome blond father, perhaps thirty-five years old, of high spirits in a country-club kind of way – daiquiris, golf and a charming (even I could feel it at ten years old) manner, with the ladies. I am quite sure the adults were having a very good time in Kahala. There was lots of drinking; certainly infidelity, although the latter was unseen by most children. The one girl in our class at Punahou whose mother had divorced was tormented unmercifully and soon turned to horses rather than schoolmates for companionship.

Christmas in the tropics was not celebrated with any less intensity than in more appropriate climates graced with snow. Santa Claus dutifully appeared, although there were no fireplaces, sweating profusely under his false beard and heavy clothing, but we did not mind the acrid odour of perspiration acquired over the years by the rented costume. Like other places, we had wreaths of holly, and mistletoe, lighted crêches, roast turkey and egg nog, and extravagant tableaux of lights in the front yards of the less elegant (and more Catholic) neighborhoods.

One Christmas Day, Mrs. Fuller, my father and three children – my brother, Rick, my younger sister and myself – fell in quickly with Mr. Fuller's giddy idea to put the big outrigger canoe on his lawn into the water – there would have been more enthusiasts, but there were only five seats in the traditional canoe; my sister, who was six, would have to sit on the bottom of the canoe, between the legs of a paddler. I had not been aware of Mr. Fuller's skill as a steersman, no easy thing with a big canoe, the work being done by a subtle but strong inflection of a paddle held in the water close to the side of the boat, but he was convincing in his Santa Claus hat with a white pompom. We pulled the canoe across the grass to the water and jumped inside, taking up the long-handled wooden paddles that all but the two younger children would

116

use. Within minutes, given the high spirits of the three adults, we were approaching the gap in the reef that led to the open sea. Although I, too, was over-excited, I sensed, despite my unworldliness, a gaiety that neared hysteria, which I now understand was stimulated by alcohol. It seemed to me then that we were joyous to excess. The weather may have contributed to the exuberance, and the holiday, of course, and the seemingly endless expanse of sea that rose before us as we glided effortlessly through the reef.

The sea was very different beyond the reef. I was delighted by the sudden change of color from grey to deep blue, and the generous troughs of water into which we were rhythmically dropped only to be lifted by the next swell. The adults, too, seemed changed by what they saw – less noisy, less easy. I was sitting in front of Mr. Fuller, in the seat (really a polished plank) called Number Four by racers, and I could hear his breathing change as he laboured to keep the canoe from swinging parallel to the waves. I saw my father look back at him once over his shoulder in what seemed to be quizzical concern as the canoe swung to the left, exposing the outrigger to an oncoming swell. A wave, larger than the others, blocked the horizon. The canoe was tilted high for one dizzying moment and we were thrown into the sea as it was overturned. I was trapped beneath the canoe for a few seconds before finally swimming free. We were not wearing life jackets. The children were quickly pulled through the water to the long floating arm of the outrigger, From my vantage point in the water, the height of the swells seemed mountainous. Mr. Fuller's red hat floated for a few minutes, then disappeared. Mrs. Fuller, never very talkative, was silent, treading water next to the children, one hand on the outrigger.

The men would have to lean their weight on the side of the overturned canoe opposite to the outrigger in the hope of flipping it over – not an easy task for two men with a large canoe. It also meant that the children would be deprived of the safety of the outrigger as it was lifted into the air. The water was cold. In busy optimism, I swam to collect the paddles that had floated away, only to be summoned back by my father's shout. It was the anger in his voice that at last made me accept that there was cause for fear.

I know from my own later excess that their drunkenness must have dissipated the moment we were in the water. The men went to work, jumping in unison to throw their weight against one rounded side of the upturned hull. It is not easy to jump in water, as everyone knows. The two children were adrift now. My sister reached out to encircle my neck. Mrs. Fuller held on to my brother, or was it he who held her afloat? I soon grew tired with the weight of my sister. I was afraid that I would vomit, and the idea seemed odd, rather like crying underwater.

My father counted to three and, with a great burst of strength, the men threw their weight onto the canoe in time with a rising swell. It took four tries, but the outrigger was raised at last, wavering tremulously as it fell gracefully into the sea. The men pulled themselves over the side. The muscles in my father's arm quivered with strain. The children and Mrs. Fuller and I were hauled over the side, and we found our way quickly to our places in the few fraught moments before the canoe was brought under control.

We bailed with cupped hands, as Mr. Fuller shakily turned the canoe towards land. With one final push from the sea, we sped back through the reef and into the familiar calm, grey water. Nothing was said, not even to those waiting unconcernedly on the beach for us. It did not make me wary of the sea, as it might have done, but wary of adults.

EMILY DICKINSON, from The Poems of Emily Dickinson

'My River runs to thee'

My River runs to thee –
Blue Sea! Wilt welcome me?
My River wait reply –
– Oh Sea – look graciously –
I'll fetch thee Brooks
From spotted nooks –
Say – Sea – Take me!

VIRGINIA WOOLF, from **The Waves**

The sun had not yet risen. The sea was indistinguishable from the sky, except that the sea was slightly creased as a cloth had wrinkles in it. Gradually as the sky whitened a dark line lay on the horizon dividing the sea from the sky and the grey cloth became barred with thick strokes moving, one after another, beneath the surface, following each other, pursuing each other, perpetually.

As they neared the shore each bar rose, heaped itself, broke and swept a thin veil of white water across the sand. The wave paused, and then drew out again, sighing like a sleeper whose breath comes and goes unconsciously. Gradually the dark bar on the horizon became clear as if the sediment in an old wine-bottle had sunk and left the glass green. Behind it, too, the sky cleared as if the white sediment there had sunk, or as if the arm of a woman couched beneath the horizon had raised a lamp and flat bars of white, green and yellow, spread across the sky like the blades of a fan. Then she raised her lamp higher and the air seemed to become fibrous and to tear away from the green surface flickering and flaming in red and yellow fibres like the smoky fire that roars from a bonfire. Gradually the fibres of the burning bonfire were fused into one haze, one incandescence which lifted the weight of the woollen grey sky on top of it and turned it to a million atoms of soft blue. The surface of the sea slowly became transparent and lay rippling and sparkling until the dark stripes were almost rubbed out. Slowly the arm that held the lamp raised it higher and then higher until a broad flame became visible; an arc of fire burnt on the rim of the horizon, and all round it the sea blazed gold.

HIS HAWAIIAN MAJESTY KING KALAKAUA, from The Legends and Myths of Hawaii

'Kelea, The Surf-Rider of Maui'

Amid a chorus of *alohas*! the canoe dashed through the

breakers and out into the open sea, holding a course in the direction of Moloka'i. Reaching that island early the next day, the party landed at Kalaupapa. The *alii nui* received them well, but inquiry led to nothing satisfactory, and, proceeding around the island, the party next landed on Lanai. It is probable that they were driven there by unfavorable winds, as Lanai was a dependency of Maui at that time, and none but subject chiefs resided on the island. However, they remained there but one day, and the next proceeded to Hana, Maui, with the intention of crossing over to Hawaii and visiting the court of Kiha at Waipio. Inquiring for the *moi*, they leaned that Kawao had removed his court from Lahaina, for the season, to Hamakuapoko, to enjoy the cool breezes of that locality and indulge in the pleasures of surf-bathing. They were further informed that a large number of chiefs had accompanied the *moi* to that attractive resort, and that Kelea, sister of the king, and the most beautiful woman on the island as well as the most daring and accomplished surf-swimmer, was also there as one of the greatest ornaments of the court.

This was agreeable information, and the party re-embarked and arrived the next morning off Hamakuapoko, just as the fair Kelea and her attendants had gone down to the beach to indulge in a buffet with the surf. Swimming out beyond the breakers, and oblivious of everything but her own enjoyment, Kelea suddenly found herself within a few yards of the canoe of the O'ahuan chiefs. Presuming that it contained her own people, she swam still closer, when she discovered, to her amazement, that all the faces in the canoe were strange to her. Perceiving her embarrassment, Kalamakua rose to his feet, and, addressing her in a courtly and respectful manner, invited her to a seat in the canoe, offering to ride the surf with it to the beach – an exciting and sometimes dangerous sport, in which great skill and coolness are required.

The language of the chief was so gentle and suggestive of the manners of the court that the invitation was accepted, and the canoe mounted one of the great waves successively following two of lighter bulk and force, and was adroitly and safely beached. The achievement was greeted with applause on the shore, and when the proposal was made to repeat the performance, Kelea willingly retained her seat. Again the canoe successfully rode the breakers ashore, and then, through her attendants, Kalamakua discovered that the fair and dashing swimmer was none other than Kelea, the sister of the *moi* of Maui.

With increased respect Kalamakua again invited his distinguished guest to join in the pleasure and excitement of a third ride over the breakers. She consented, and the canoe was once more pulled out beyond the surf, where it remained for a moment, awaiting a high, combing roller on which to be borne to the landing. One passed and was missed, and before another came a squall, or what was called a *mumuku*, suddenly struck the canoe, rendering it utterly unmanageable and driving it out upon the broad ocean.

When the canoe started Kelea would have leaped into the sea had she not been restrained; but Kalamakua spoke so kindly to her – assuring her that they would safely ride out the storm and return to Hamakuapoko – that she became calmer, and consented to curl down beside him in the boat to escape the fury of the winds. Her shapely limbs and shoulders were bare, and her hair, braided and bound loosely back, was still wet, and grew chilling in the wind where it fell. Kalamakua took from a covered calabash a handsome *kihei*, or mantle, and wrapped it around her shoulders, and then seated her in the shelter of his own burly form. She smiled her thanks for these delicate attentions, and the chief was compelled to admit to himself that the reports of her great beauty had not been exaggerated. He could recall no maiden on O'ahu who was her equal in grace and comeliness, and felt that could she be secured for his eccentric cousin, his search would be at an end. He even grew indignant at the thought that she might not prove acceptable, but smiled the next moment at his promise to marry the girl himself should she be refused by his cousin.

But the fierce *mumuku* afforded him but little time to indulge such dreams. The sea surged in fury, and like a cockleshell the canoe was tossed from one huge wave to another. The spray was almost blinding, and, while Kalamakua kept the little craft squarely before the wind as a measure of first importance, his companions were earnestly employed in alternately bailing and trimming as emergency suggested.

On, on sped the canoe, farther and farther out into the open sea, tossed like a feather by the crested waves and pelted by the driving spray. The scene was fearful. The southern skies had grown black with wrath, and long streamers sent from the clouds shot northward as if to surround and cut off the retreat of the flying craft. All crouched in the bottom of the boat, intent only on keeping it before the wind and preventing it from filling. A frailer craft would have been stove to pieces; but it was hewn from the truck of a sound *koa* tree, and gallantly rode out the storm.

But when the wind ceased and the skies cleared, late in the afternoon, the canoe was far out at sea and beyond the sight of land. It was turned and headed back but as there was no wind to assist the paddles and the waters were still rough and restless, slow progress toward land was made; and when the sun went down Kalamakua was undecided which way to proceed,

127

as he was not certain that the storm had not carried them so far from the coast of Maui that some point on Moloka'i or O'ahu might be more speedily and safely reached than the place from which they started. Their supply of *poi* had been lost during the gale by the breaking of the vessel containing it; but they had still left a small quantity of dried fish, raw potatoes and bananas, and a calabash of water, and ate their evening meal as cheerfully as if their supplies were exhaustless and the green hills of Waialua smiled upon them in the distance. Such was the Hawaiian of the past; such is the Hawaiian of today. His joys and griefs are centred in the present, and he broods but little over the past, and borrows no trouble from the future.

The stars came out, and a light wind began to steal down upon them from the northwest. It was quite chilly, and felt like the breath of the returning trade-winds, which start from the frozen shores of northwestern America, and gradually grow warmer as they sweep down through the tropic seas. These winds, continuing, with intervals of cessation, eight or nine months in the year, are what give life, beauty and an endurable climate to the Hawaiian group.

As the breeze freshened sails were raised, and then the course to be taken remained to be determined. Kalamakua expressed his doubts to Kelea, as if inviting a suggestion from her; but she was unable to offer any advice, declaring that she had not noticed the course of the wind that had driven them so far out upon the ocean.

'And I am equally in doubt,' said the chief. 'We may have been blown farther toward the rising of the sun than the headlands of Hana. If so, the course we are now sailing would take us to Hawaii, if not, indeed, beyond, while in following the evening star we might even pass O'ahu. I therefore suggest a course between these two directions, which will certainly bring us to land some time to-morrow.'

'Then, since we are all in doubt,' replied Kelea, 'and the winds are blowing landward, why not trust to the gods and follow them?'

JOHN KEATS, from The Poetical Works

'On the Sea'

It keeps eternal whisperings around
    Desolate shores, and with its mighty
        swell
    Gluts twice ten thousand caverns; till
        the spell
Of Hecate leaves them their old shadowy
  sound.
Often 'tis in such gentle temper found
    That scarcely will the very smallest shell
    Be moved for days from whence it
        sometime fell,
When last the winds of heaven were
  unbound.
O ye who have your eyeballs vext and tir'd,
    Feast them upon the wideness of the sea;
O ye whose ears are dinned with uproar
  rude, or fed too much with cloying
  melody –

Sit ye near some old cavern's mouth and
   brood
Until ye start, as if the sea nymphs
   quired.

WILKIE COLLINS, *from* The Moonstone

Our house is high up on the Yorkshire coast, and close
by the sea. We have got beautiful walks all round us,
in every direction but one. That one I acknowledge
to be a horrid walk. It leads, for a quarter of a mile,
through a melancholy plantation of firs, and brings
you out between low cliffs on the loneliest and ugliest
little bay on all our coast.

The sand-hills here are run down to the sea, and
end in two spits of rock jutting out opposite each
other, till you lose sight of them in the water. One
is called the North Spit, and one called the South.
Between the two, shifting backwards and forwards
at certain seasons of the year, lies the most horrible

quicksand on the shores of Yorkshire. At the turn of the tide, something goes on in the unknown deeps below, which sets the whole face of the quicksand shivering and trembling in a manner most remarkable to see, and which has given to it, among the people in our parts, the name of The Shivering Sand. A great bank, half a mile out, nigh the mouth of the bay, breaks the force of the main ocean coming in from the offing. Winter and summer, when the tide flows over the quicksand, the sea seems to leave the waves behind it on the bank, and rolls its waters in smoothly with a heave, and covers the sand in silence. A lonesome and a horrid retreat, I can tell you! No boat ever ventures into this bay. No children from our fishing-village, called Cobb's Hole, ever come here to play. The very birds of the air, as it seems to me, give the Shivering Sand a wide berth. That a young woman, with dozens of nice walks to choose from, and company to go with her, if she only said 'Come!' should prefer this place, and should sit and work or read in it, all alone, when it's her turn out, I grant you, passes belief.

ROBERT LOUIS STEVENSON, *from*
Treasure Island

The coracle – as I had ample reason to know before I was done with her – was a very safe boat for a person of my height and weight, both buoyant and clever in a sea-way; but she was the most cross-grained, lop-sided craft to manage. Do as you pleased, she always made more leeway than anything else, and turning round and round was the manoeuvre she was best at. Even Ben Gunn himself has admitted that she was 'queer to handle till you knew her way'.

Certainly I did not know her way. She turned in every direction but the one I was bound to go; the most part of the time we were broadside on, and I am very sure I never should have made the ship at all but for the tide. By good fortune, paddle as I pleased, the tide was still sweeping me down; and there lay the *Hispaniola* right in the fairway, hardly to be missed.

First she loomed before me like a blot of something yet blacker than darkness, then her spars and hull began to take shape, and the next moment, as it seemed (for, the farther I went, the brisker grew the current of the ebb), I was alongside of her hawser and had laid hold.

The hawser was as taut as a bowstring, and the current so strong she pulled upon her anchor. All round the hull, in the blackness, the rippling current bubbled and chattered like a little mountain stream. One cut with my sea-gully and the *Hispaniola* would go humming down the tide.

So far so good, but it next occurred to my recollection that a taut hawser, suddenly cut, is a thing as dangerous as a kicking horse. Ten to one, if I were so foolhardy as to cut the *Hispaniola* from her anchor, I and the coracle would be knocked clean out of the water.

This brought me to a full stop, and if fortune had not again particularly favoured me, I should have had to abandon my design. But the light airs which had begun blowing from the south-east and south had hauled round after nightfall into the south-west. Just while I was meditating, a puff came, caught the *Hispaniola*, and forced her up into the current; and to my great joy, I felt the hawser slacken in my grasp, and the hand by which I held it dip for a second under water.

With that I made my mind up, took out my gully, opened it with my teeth, and cut one strand after another, fill the vessel swung only by two. Then I lay quiet, waiting to sever these last when the strain should be once more lightened by a breath of wind.

All this time I had heard the sound of loud voices from the cabin, but to say truth, my mind had been so entirely taken up with other thoughts that I had scarcely given ear. Now, however, when I had nothing else to do, I began to pay more heed.

One I recognized for the coxswain's, Israel Hands, that had been Flint's gunner in former days. The other was, of course, my friend of the red nightcap. Both men were plainly the worse of drink, and they were still drinking, for even while I was listening, one of them, with a drunken cry, opened the stern window and threw out something, which I divined to be an empty bottle. But they were not only tipsy; it was plain that they were furiously angry. Oaths flew like hailstones, and every now and then there came forth such an explosion as I thought was sure to end in blows. But each time the quarrel passed off and the voices grumbled lower for a while, until the next crisis came and in its turn passed away without result.

On shore, I could see the glow of the great campfire burning warmly through the shore-side trees. Someone was singing, a dull, old, droning sailor's song, with a droop and a quaver at the end of every verse, and seemingly no end to it at all but the patience of the singer. I had heard it on the voyage more than once and remembered these words:

> 'But one man of her crew alive,
> What put to sea with seventy-five.'

And I thought it was a ditty rather too dolefully appropriate for a company that had met such cruel losses in the morning. But, indeed, from what I saw, all these buccaneers were as callous as the sea they sailed on.

At last the breeze came; the schooner sidled and drew nearer in the dark, I felt the hawser slacken once more, and with a good, tough effort, cut the last fibres through.

The breeze had but little action on the coracle, and I was almost instantly swept against the bows of the *Hispaniola*. At the same time, the schooner began to turn upon her heel, spinning slowly, end for end, across the current.

I wrought like a fiend, for I expected every moment to be swamped; and since I found I could not push the coracle directly off, I now shoved straight astern. At length I was clear of my dangerous neighbour, and just as I gave the last impulsion, my hands came across a light cord that was tailing overboard across the stern bulwarks. Instantly I grasped it.

Why I should have done so I can hardly say. It was at first mere instinct, but once I had it in my hands and found it fast, curiosity began to get the upper hand, and I determined I should have one look through the cabin window.

I pulled in hand over hand on the cord, and when I judged myself near enough, rose at infinite risk to about half my height and thus commanded the roof and a slice of the interior of the cabin.

By this time the schooner and her little consort were gliding pretty swiftly through the water; indeed, we had already fetched up level with the camp-fire. The ship was talking, as sailors say, loudly, treading the innumerable ripples with an incessant weltering splash; and until I got my eye above the window-sill I could not comprehend why the watchmen had taken no alarm. One glance, however, was sufficient; and it was only one glance that I durst take from that unsteady skiff. It showed me Hands and his companion locked together in deadly wrestle, each with a hand upon the other's throat.

I dropped upon the thwart again, none too soon, for I was near overboard. I could see nothing for the moment but these two furious, encrimsoned faces swaying together under the smoky lamp, and I shut my eyes to let them grow once more familiar with the darkness.

The endless ballad had come to an end at last, and the whole diminished company about the camp-fire had broken into the chorus I had heard so often:

> 'Fifteen men on the dead man's chest
> Yo-ho-ho, and a bottle of rum!
> Drink and the devil had done for the rest
> Yo-ho-ho, and a bottle of rum!'

I was just thinking how busy drink and the devil were at that very moment in the cabin of the *Hispaniola* when I was surprised by a sudden lurch of the coracle. At the same moment, she yawed sharply and seemed to change her course. The speed in the meantime had strangely increased.

I opened my eyes at once. All round me were little ripples, combing over with a sharp, bristling sound and slightly phosphorescent. The *Hispaniola* herself, a few yards in whose wake I was still being whirled along, seemed to stagger in her course, and I saw her spars toss a little against the blackness of the night; nay, as I looked longer, I made sure she also was wheeling to the southward.

I glanced over my shoulder, and my heart jumped against my ribs. There, right behind me, was the glow of the camp-fire. The current had turned at right angles, sweeping round along with it the tall schooner and the little dancing coracle; ever quickening, ever bubbling higher, ever muttering louder, it went spitting through the narrows for the open sea.

Suddenly the schooner in front of me gave a violent yaw, turning, perhaps, through twenty degrees; and almost at the same moment one shout followed another from on board; I could hear feet pounding on the companion ladder and I knew that the two drunkards had at last been interrupted in their quarrel and awakened to a sense of their disaster.

I lay down flat in the bottom of that wretched skiff and devoutly recommended my spirit to its Maker. At the end of the straits, I made sure we must fail into some bar of raging breakers, where all my troubles would be ended speedily; and though I could, perhaps, bear to die, I could not bear to look upon my fate as it approached. So I must have lain for hours, continually beaten to and fro upon the billows, now and again wetted with flying sprays, and never ceasing to expect death at the next plunge. Gradually weariness grew upon me; a numbness, an occasional stupor, fell upon my mind even in the midst of my terrors, until sleep at last supervened and in my sea-tossed coracle I lay and dreamed of home and the old Admiral Benbow.

HENRY DAVID THOREAU, from
Cape Cod

The brig *St John*, from Galway, Ireland, laden with Emigrants, was wrecked on Sunday morning; it was now Tuesday morning, and the sea was still breaking violently on the rocks. There were eighteen or twenty of the same large boxes that I have mentioned, lying on a green hill-side, a few rods from the water, and surrounded by a crowd. The bodies which had been recovered, twenty-seven or -eight in all, had been collected there. Some were rapidly nailing down the lids, other were carting the boxes away, and others were lifting the lids, which were yet loose, and peeping under the cloths, for each body, with such rags as still adhered to it, was covered loosely with a white sheet. I witnessed no signs of grief but there was a sober despatch of business which was affecting. One man was seeking to identify a particular body, and one undertaker or carpenter was calling to another to know in what box a certain child was put. I saw many marble feet and matted heads as the cloths were raised, and one livid, swollen, and mangled body of a drowned girl, who probably had intended to go out to service in some American family, to which some rags still adhered, with a string, half concealed by the flesh, about its swollen neck; the coiled-up wreck of a human hulk, gashed by the rocks or fishes, so that the bone and muscle were exposed, but quite bloodless, – merely red and white, – with wide-open and staring eyes, yet lustreless, dead-lights; or like the cabin windows of a stranded vessel, filled with sand. Sometimes there were two or more children, or a parent and child, in the same box, and on the lid would perhaps be written with red chalk, 'Bridget such-a-one, and sister's child'. The surrounding sward was covered with bits of sails and clothing. I have since heard, from one who lives by this beach, that a woman who had come over before, but had left her infant behind for her sister to bring, came and looked into these boxes, and saw in one – probably the same whose superscription I have quoted, – her child in her sister's arms, as if the sister had meant to be found thus; and within three days after the mother died from the effect of that sight.

We turned from this and walked along the rocky shore. In the first cove were strewn what seemed the fragments of a vessel, in small pieces mixed with sand and sea-weed, and great quantities of feathers; but it looked so old and rusty, that I at first took it to be some old wreck which had lain there many years. I even thought of Captain Kidd and that the feathers were those which sea-fowl had cast there; and perhaps there might be some tradition about it in the neighborhood. I asked a sailor if that was the *St. John*. He said it was. I asked him where she struck. He pointed to a rock in front of us, a mile from the shore, called the Grampus Rock …

About a mile south we could see, rising above the rocks, the masts of the British brig which the *St. John* had endeavored to follow, which had slipped her cables, and, by good luck, run into the mouth of Cobasset Harbor.

A little further along the shore we saw a man's clothes on a rock; further, a woman's scarf, a gown, a straw bonnet, the brig's caboose, and one of her masts high and dry, broken into several pieces. In another rocky cove, several rods from the water, and behind rocks twenty feet high, lay a part of one side of the vessel, still hanging together. It was, perhaps, forty feet long, by fourteen wide. I was even more surprised at the power of the waves, exhibited on this shattered fragment, than I had been at the sight of the smaller fragments before. The largest timbers and iron braces were broken superfluously, and I saw that no material could withstand the power of the waves; that iron must go to pieces in such a case, and an iron vessel would be cracked up like an egg-shell on the rocks.

Some of these timbers, however, were so rotten that I could almost thrust my umbrella through them. They told us that some were saved on this piece, and also showed where the sea had heaved it into this cove, which was now dry. When I saw where it had come in, and in what condition, I wondered that any had been saved on it. A little further on a crowd of men was collecting around the mate of the *St. John*, who was telling his story. He was a slim-looking youth, who spoke of the captain as the master, and seemed a little excited. He was saying that when they jumped into the boat, she filled, and, the vessel lurching, the weight of the water in the boat caused the painter to break, and so they were separated.

ANTON CHEKHOV, from Notebook

A storm at sea. Lawyers ought to regard it as a crime.

WASHINGTON IRVING, *from*
The Sketchbook of Geoffrey Crayon, Gent.

'The Voyage'

We one day described some shapeless object drifting at a distance. At sea every thing that breaks the monotony of the surrounding expanse attracts attention. It proved to be the mast of a ship that must have been completely wrecked; for there were the remains of handkerchiefs, by which some of the crew had fastened themselves to this spar to prevent their being washed off by the waves. There was no trace by which the name of the ship could be ascertained. The wreck had evidently drifted about for many months: clusters of shell-fish had fastened about it and long sea weeds flaunted at its sides.

But where, thought I, is the crew! – Their struggle has long been over – they have gone down amidst the roar of the tempest – their bones lie whitening among the caverns of the deep. Silence – oblivion, like the waves, have closed over them, and no one can tell the story of their end. What sighs have been wafted after that ship; what prayers offered up at the deserted fireside of home ...

... The sight of this wreck, as usual, gave rise to many dismal anecdotes. This was particularly the case in the evening when the weather, which had hitherto been fair, began to look wild and threatening, and gave indications of one of those sudden storms which will sometimes break in upon the serenity of a summer voyage. As we sat round the dull light of a lamp in the cabin, that made the gloom more ghastly, every one had his tale of shipwreck and disaster. I was peculiarly struck with a short one related by the captain.

'As I was once sailing,' said he, 'in a fine stout ship across the banks of Newfoundland, one of those heavy fogs which prevail in those parts rendered it impossible for us to see far ahead even in the day time; but at night the weather was so thick that we could not distinguish any object at twice the length of the ship. I kept lights at the mast head and a constant watch forward to look out for fishing smacks, which are accustomed to lie at anchor on the banks. The wind was blowing a smacking breeze and we were going at a great rate through the water. Suddenly the watch gave the alarm of "a sail ahead!" – it was scarcely uttered before we were upon her. She was a small schooner at anchor, with the broad side toward us. The crew were all asleep, and had neglected to hoist a light. We struck her just a mid-ships. The force, the size and weight of our vessel bore her down below the waves – we passed over her and were hurried on our course. As the crashing wreck was sinking beneath us I had a glimpse of two or three half-naked wretches, rushing from her cabin – they just started from their beds to be swallowed shrieking by the waves. I heard their drowning cry mingling with the wind. The blast that bore it to our ears swept us out of all further hearing – I shall never forget that cry! – It was some time before we could put the ship about; she was under such headway. We returned as nearly as we could guess to the place where the smack had anchored. We cruised about for several hours in the dense fog. We fired signal guns and listened if we might hear the halloo of any survivors; but all was silent – we never saw or heard any thing of them more! –'

VI

Being at sea is so queer

A few years ago I spent a month on a ranch on the top of a hill at the far eastern end of the island of Moloka'i overlooking the bay of Halawa. The road goes no farther than Pu'u O Hoku, the 'hill of stars'. It is cool at night, and there is the sound of the wind moving through the ironwood, bringing the scent of eucalyptus. There are cattle on the mountainside, and horses and small animals – rats and mongoose, toads and bats. Halawa, once a large fishing and farming village, flourished in the 10th century. A river fed by numerous waterfalls winds through a narrow valley overgrown with guava, banana, coffee bushes, and ginger. A short distance into the forest, there are traces of taro patches and house foundations, and the stone ruins of altars and shrines. '[Papa *heiau*] ... is a

149

rambling structure,' according to the Moloka'i Site Survey. 'A collection of small platforms, terraces and walls, suggesting more the site of a college of priests than a *heiau* ... Located on the northern side of Halawa Valley, [Mana *heiau*] is by far the most imposing *heiau* structure in the valley ... [Built by the *menehune*], it was for human sacrifice.'

Moloka'i is small (only thirty-seven miles from west to east; ten miles in width), and the population remains much what it has been for two hundred years, perhaps five thousand people. The land is forested or used for agriculture. The first Protestant mission was founded in 1832. The use of an inaccessible peninsula on the north shore for the leper colony, Kalaupapa, has added to the island's mystery and its isolation, despite its nickname, 'The Friendly Isle', surely a fantasy of the Visitors' Bureau. Kaunakaka'i, the capital, is a dusty cowboy town of a few hundred people with three streets of wooden buildings with false pediments. A hotel, now closed, did not open on the dry west end until 1977.

For some years, I have sought the sacred grove,

Ulukuku' o Lanikaula, on my walks along the cliff overlooking the sea, but I have never been fully satisfied that I've found the exact place of the seer Lanikaula's encampment, said to be a luminous grove of the silver-leafed *kuku'i* or candlenut tree. Lanikaula was a sorcerer of Maui who sought refuge on Moloka'i in the 16th century. He is said to be buried in the *kuku'i* grove. 'Here he lived in seclusion and acquired a great reputation as a prophet and counsellor, so that from all the group [of islands], pilgrims came to the grove to seek advice and register vows; the latter process consisted in cutting a gash in one of the *kuku'i* trees forming the grove, and in the slit placing a lock of the votary's hair which was soon cemented there by the gum exuded by the tree.' The *kuku'i* tree is sacred to the Hawaiians and the source of endless gifts to them. The hollowed nuts were filled with their own oil and strung in a line on stiff fronds, burning for a minute or two before extinguishing themselves one by one. The leaves and bark were used for medicine; the inner bark made a permanent blood-red dye and a gum secreted by the tree was used to varnish *kapa* cloth. The black or mottled-brown nuts are still highly polished and strung on black ribbon for sale in tourist shops.

I have also spent years looking for the Vagina Rock that is companion to the splendid Phallic Rock in the mountains, but the Vagina Rock has been so long abandoned in a thicket of cedar, so overgrown with roots that I fear it is lost forever. 'If you pass through Kualapu'u to the forest,' says the local storyteller Harriet Ne, 'you can see the great rock six feet high which is called Kaule o Nanahoa, which means the "penis of Nanahoa". Nanahoa was a prince who ... protected the rock because it was on his property. Also, it was precious to his people because it was known to cure infertility. But for him – and not only for him – it was a sorrow. He was married to a beautiful woman, and they were very happy until another woman came from another district. Nanahoa did not resist her loving glances, and soon they became lovers. The heart of his wife burned hotly within her; and when she found them together at the rock, she cried out in rage and hurled bitter accusations at them. Then she sprang at the woman and pushed her down the cliff. Even today, if you go there, you will find a perfectly formed female rock. I myself have seen it.' I have not.

One late afternoon friends and I set out, once again, to find the place of Lanikaula's sacred grove on our three-mile walk to the bird sanctuary. The family to whom Pu'u O Hoku belongs has established a sanctuary on a grassy bluff overlooking the Cape of Halawa for the endangered *nene* goose, one of the few animals known to be endemic to the Islands. On the verge of extinction in the 1940s, much attention, some of it sentimental, has been given to saving the idiosyncratic little goose. One of its virtues is its ability to make its home on lava, without a source of water. It does not have much webbing between its toes.

I had begged more detailed directions from the Hawaiian woman who looked after us. Surprised that I was having so much trouble finding the grove, she explained once again: 'Go up the cattle road, through the eucalyptus, take the down fork when you reach the bend and there it is.' I had done that many times, and still I had not come upon the sacred grove. This time, however, she let slip an additional detail: 'There is an old fence around it.'

In Greek myth, Pasiphaë, She Who Shines for All, the wife of the Cretan king, Minos, beseeched of the exiled Daedalus, a sculptor of inventions and maker of toys for the royal children (among them Ariadne), a sculpture of a cow into which Pasiphaë could fit herself. She had fallen in love with a beautiful white bull and could not rid herself of a consuming passion for it. Daedalus obliged her in secret, making a lovely cow in which Pasiphaë could conceal herself. The cow with Pasiphaë inside was placed in a field and soon gained the notice of the beautiful white bull. He mounted the cow again and again, thus giving the queen the pleasure and release that her feverish desire required. In time, a child she conceived with the bull was born, the Minotaur, who possessed the body of a man and the head of a bull. Shamed by this proof of his wife's betrayal, Minos had Daedalus contrive a labyrinth in which the Minotaur could be imprisoned. (Although the myth of Pasiphaë and the bull is a metaphor for the ritual marriage held under an oak tree to affirm the union of the moon-priestess, wearing a diadem of cow's horns, and the Minos-king, wearing a mask to resemble a bull, and the labyrinth is thought to be Minos's enormous palace in Cnossus with its many doors and winding passages, I choose to believe in the Minotaur.)

I had walked past the grove many times – I'd rested beside it, and once fallen asleep in the weedy field that surrounds it. The *kuku'i* is not a rare tree and it is easily seen from a distance thanks to its silver leaves. I had imagined that the sacred grove would announce itself in a blaze of light and a rustling of spirits, but the grove was commonplace. The barbed-wire fence was partly obscured by brush, but even had the grove been in the open, it did not appear distinguished. Certainly not sacred. What a lovely trick!

That afternoon, my friend Kiki was wearing, as she tends to do, a pleated black Issey Miyake dress that reached to her ankles, thin sandals and the heavy, jingling silver anklets of an Indian *apsara*. I was wearing khaki breeches in anticipation of riding with the cowboys. My friend, John Newman, a sculptor, and my daughter, Lulu, in a white nightgown, having just awakened, walked with us.

The fence around the field was so old that the rust rubbed off on my palms when I held down the knotted wire so that the others could step over it. Lulu had a moment's difficulty, but only because of her flowing raiment. We walked through the field, the high grass twitching with wasps. There was yet another fence around the dark grove itself, but it was made of rotten boughs, and there was a gate without a lock. I pushed open the gate and we entered the labyrinth.

The trees, scarred with nicks from generations of propitiations, were old, the trunks bound with pale strands of desiccated moss. Although it was not the season, one yellow guava glimmered on a tree with mottled bark and spindly arms, its leaves *hinahina*, gray and withered. I had been longing for guavas, like the woman who craved rampion in 'Rapunzel'. As I went to pick the guava, there was the sound of breaking boughs and a terrible scream. It sounded like

156

a woman in pain; a woman murdered. A long-horned bull pushed his way noisily through the *kuku'i* and planted himself, legs splayed, head lowered, before us. I put my hand in my pocket to hold tight to the lock of hair I had cut from my head as an offering, but Kiki, her anklets silent for once beneath her black gown, reached to pick the guava. The wild bull watched us, stiff-legged, moaning with rage. The tree trembled as it resisted Kiki's pull, but at last gave up the little fruit with a shudder. John, never taking his eyes from the bull, walked backward through the trees, silently finding his way to the gate which he held open for us.

The guava clutched in her hand, Kiki bounded through the trees, clearing the fence as gracefully as one of the evening deer who stood in the far field, watching us without fear or interest. I dropped the lock of hair as Lulu grabbed my hand. A shrieking bird flitted indignantly above our heads, perhaps the *'aumakua* of Lanikaula, the *o'o* that cries out in warning when strangers venture too near. The wild bull bellowed in the trees as we ran through the dusk.

We sat on the bank of ferns by the side of the

157

cattle road to catch our breath. John and Kiki would not share the guava, insisting that I have it. Lulu and I ate the guava in four quick bites. Delicious.

D. H. LAWRENCE, from the Letters

R. M. S. 'Osterley'
Wednesday, 8 March 1922

My dear Rosalind –
Here we are on this ship – ten days at sea. It is rather lovely – perfect weather all the time, ship steady as can be, enough wind now to keep it cool. We went on shore at Port Said – and it's still like Arabian Nights, spite of all. Then I loved coming through the Suez Canal – five miles an hour. You see the desert, the sandhills, the low palm trees, Arabs with camels working at the side. I like it so much. Now we are in the Arabian Sea and expect to come to Colombo on Monday morning: 15 days' voyage.

The ship is so pleasant – only about half full – or less – so plenty of room. We have come second class, and it is perfectly comfortable and nice, couldn't want anything better. Alas, it came to 140 pounds for the two of us. But I had to get out of Europe. In Ceylon we stay with friends. There are children on board having the time of their lives. I am translating Verga's *Mastro don Gesualdo*, to pass the time. By the way I should be so glad if you would some time send me an old Italian novel or book that you have done with – if it is interesting. I should like to go on reading Italian. The people on board are mostly simple Australians. I believe Australia is a good country, full of life and energy. I believe that is the country for you if you had anything specific in mind. If we don't want to go on living in Ceylon I shall go to Australia if we can manage it.

I ordered you *Sea and Sardinia* and *Tortoises* I hope you will get them – the former from England, Secker, the latter from America, which takes a long time.

Being at sea is so queer – it sort of dissolves for the time being all the connexions with the land, and one feels a bit like a sea-bird must feel. It is my opinion that once beyond the Red Sea one does not feel any more that tension and pressure one suffers from in England – in Europe altogether – even in America, I believe – perhaps worse there. I feel so glad I have come out, but don't know how the money is going to behave. Can't help it.

Write and tell me all that happens – 'Ardnaree,' Lake View Estate, Kandy, Ceylon. It seems difficult in the world to get a new *start* – so much easier to make more ends. F. sends many greetings – she is a bit dazed by the sea.

ISABELLA BIRD, from
Six Months in the Sandwich Islands

Steamer *Nevada*, North Pacific, January 19th, 1873

... taking a boat at a wharf, in whose seams the pitch was melting, I went off to the steamer *Nevada*, which was anchored out in the bay, preferring to spend the night in her than in the unbearable heat on shore (Auckland). She belongs to the Webb line, an independent mail adventure, now dying a natural death, undertaken by the New Zealand Government, as much probably out of jealousy of Victoria as anything else. She nearly foundered on her last voyage, and her passengers unanimously signed a protest against her unseaworthy condition. She was condemned by the Government surveyor, and her mails were sent to Melbourne. She has, however, been patched up for this trip, and eight passengers, including myself, have trusted ourselves to her. She is a huge paddle-steamer, of the old-fashioned American type, deck above deck, balconies, a pilot-house abaft the foremast, two monstrous walking beams, and two masts which, possibly in case of need, might serve as jury masts.

Huge, airy, perfectly comfortable as she is, not a passenger stepped on board without breathing a more earnest prayer than usual that the voyage might end propitiously. The very first evening statements were whispered about to the effect that her state of

161

disrepair is such that she has not been to her own port for nine months, and has been sailing for that time without a certificate; that her starboard shaft is partially fractured, and that to reduce the strain upon it the floats of her starboard wheel have been shortened five inches, the strain being further reduced by giving her a decided list to port, that her crank is 'bandaged', that she is leaky, that her mainmast is sprung, and that with only four hours' steaming many of her boiler tubes, even some of those put in at Auckland, had already given way. I cannot testify concerning the mainmast though it certainly does comport itself like no other mainmast I ever saw; but the other statements, and many more which might be added, are, I believe, substantially correct. That the caulking of the deck was in evil case we very soon had proof, for heavy rain on deck was a smart shower in the saloon and state rooms, keeping four stewards employed with buckets and swabs, and compelling us to dine in waterproofs and rubber shoes.

In this dilapidated condition, when two days out from Auckland, we encountered a revolving South

Sea hurricane, succinctly entered in the log of the day as 'Encountered a very severe hurricane with a very heavy sea'. It began at eight in the morning, and never spent its fury till nine at night, and the wind changed its direction eleven times. The *Nevada* left Auckland two feet deeper in the water than she ought to have been, and laboured heavily. Seas smack her under the guards with a heavy, explosive *thud*, and she groaned and strained as if she would part asunder. We held no communication with each other, or with those who could form any rational estimate of the probabilities of our destiny; no officials appeared; the ordinary invariable routine of the steward department was suspended without notice; the sounds were tremendous, and a hot, lurid obscurity filled the atmosphere. Soon after four the clamour increased, and the shock of a sea blowing up a part of the fore-guards made the groaning fabric reel and shiver throughout her whole bulk. At that time, by common consent, we assembled in the deck-house, which had windows looking in all directions, and sat there for five hours. Very few words were spoken, and very little fear was felt. We understood by intuition that if our crazy engines failed at any moment to keep the ship's head to the sea, her destruction would not occupy half an hour. It was all palpable. There was nothing which the most experienced seamen could explain to the merest novice. We hoped for the best, and there was no use in speaking about the worse. Nor, indeed, was speech possible, unless a human voice could have out-shrieked the hurricane.

In this deck-house the strainings, sunderings, and groaning were hardly audible, or rather were overpowered by a sound which, in thirteen months' experience of the sea in all weathers, I have never heard, and hope never to hear again, unless in a staunch ship, one loud, awful, undying shriek, mingled with a prolonged, relentless hiss. No gathering strength, no languid fainting into momentary lulls, but one protracted, gigantic scream. And this was not the whistle of wind through cordage, but the actual sound of air travelling with tremendous velocity, carrying with it minute particles of water. Nor was the sea running mountains high, for the hurricane kept it down. Indeed during those fierce hours no sea was visible, for the whole surface was caught up and carried furiously into the air, like snow-drift on the prairies, sibilant, relentless. There was profound quiet on deck, the little life which existed being concentrated near the bow, where the captain was either lashed to the foremast, or in shelter of the pilot-house. Never a soul appeared on deck, the force of the hurricane being such that for four hours any man would have been carried off his feet. Through the swift strange evening our hopes rested on the engine, and amidst the uproar and din, and drifting spray, and shocks of pitiless seas, there was a sublime repose in the spectacle of the huge walking beams, alternately rising and falling, slowly, calmly, regularly, as if the *Nevada* were on a holiday trip within the Golden Gate. At eight in the evening we could hear each other speak and a little later, through the great masses of hissing drift we discerned black water. At nine Captain Blethen appeared, smoking a cigar with nonchalance, and told us that the hurricane had nearly boxed the compass, and had been the most severe he had known for seventeen years. This grand old man, nearly the oldest captain in the Pacific, won our respect and confidence from the first, and his quiet and masterly handling of this dilapidated old ship is beyond all praise.

HESIOD, from Works and Days

Fifty days after the solstice, when the season of wearisome heat is come to an end, is the right time for men to go sailing. Then you will not wreck your ship, nor will the sea destroy the sailors, unless Poseidon the Earth-Shaker be set upon it, or Zeus, the king of the deathless gods, wish to slay them; for the issues of good and evil are alike with them. At that time the winds are steady, and the sea is harmless. Then trust in the winds without care, and haul your swift ship down to the sea and put all the freight on board; but make all haste you can to return home again and do not wait till the time of the new wine and autumn rain and oncoming storms with the fierce gales of Notus who accompanies the autumn rains of Zeus and stirs up the sea and makes the deep dangerous.

Another time for men to go sailing is in spring when a man first sees leaves on the topmost shoot of a fig tree as large as the foot-print that a crow makes; then the sea is passable, and this is the spring sailing time. For my part I do not praise it, for my heart does not like it. Such a sailing is snatched, and you will hardly avoid mischief. Yet in their ignorance men do even this, for wealth means life to poor mortals; but it is fearful to die among the waves. But I bid you consider all these things in your heart as I say. Do not put all your goods in hollow ships; leave the greater part behind, and put the lesser part on board; for it is a bad business to meet with disaster among the waves of the sea, as it is bad if you put too great a load on your wagon and break the axle, and your goods are spoiled. Observe due measure: and proportion is best in all things.

RACHEL HENNING, from
The Letters of Rachel Henning

'Great Britain' Sunday, February 17th, 1861

My Dearest Etta,

You will be surprised to hear from me again, as no doubt you are thinking today that I am half-way down the Irish Channel; but, although we seemed to start yesterday, the ship only went a short distance down the river and then anchored again. There was some hitch about her papers, the captain said.

... After I sent off my letter yesterday, we were called to dinner. By the steward's advice Mrs. Bronchordt and I sat down at the top of the captain's table next him, but I do not think that otherwise we have got among a very interesting set of people. There are several commercial gentlemen, or rather not gentlemen, and a little Scotchman, who looks more polished, also a pretty German, wife to one of the commercials, and who cannot speak a word of English. They are all very civil and unoffending, however.

The first evening was sure to be rather dull and dismal. However, we got books and sat round a candle in the saloon (where they have candles in dishes instead of lamps. I should think, in rough weather, the consequences would be disastrous), till nine o'clock, when Mrs. Bronchordt and myself betook ourselves to bed.

I had been busy all day arranging my goods, so everything came to hand very easily, and Mrs. Bronchordt is very civil and accommodating. I think we shall get on very nicely.

The cabin is so light that I can read well in bed, and the lamp shines into my berth, so, that being the case, I have nailed up a moreen bag just within reach of my hand, and put a little store of books into it; also my lantern matches, camphor, etc.

It was not to be expected that we should sleep very soundly the first night, especially as a baby cried in the next cabin considerably. What a life its poor mother will have when we get to sea and she and the children are all seasick! Of course the ship is now as steady as possible, but that will not last long. The stewardess called us at eight and brought a jug of hot

169

water, an unexpected luxury, and we managed about dressing very well, as I got up first.

I am so well provided with everything I want that there never seems any difficulty; my dress and jacket are warm and comfortable and everything just right. How nicely you helped me in all that shopping. The bag of tools is worth its weight in gold. I have driven innumerable nails for Mrs. Bronchordt and myself, and though the steward did come and inquire if the carpenter was in our cabin yesterday, as he was particularly wanted, no one has found any fault with the nails, and the cupboard which Mr. Boyce screwed up behind the funnel has never been seen and is most useful.

They do not feed you so well on board this ship as they did in the *Calcutta*. There is a quantity of food, but it is coarse; great joints of pork and underdone mutton and chiefly cold. However, the first day is not a fair sample, and when the captain is on board and we are fairly off, no doubt all will go on smoother. I have not seen Captain Gray since I came on board yesterday. They say he is to come off at twelve, and that we shall sail with the top of the tide at three today.

... I am very well content, dear, though a little lonely. There is nothing to complain of in the ship or passengers so far, though I do not see many who *look* as if I should care about them. Mrs. Bronchordt is very kind and pleasant, but I do not think there is much in her.

I am writing in the saloon, after breakfast, with a great many people writing round me, for the last mail ...

... The 'ladies' boudoir' which they talk about is a nice little room enough, but rather dark and chiefly used by the children. I shall probably sit in the saloon, most likely where I am sitting now by the table just opposite the entrance to my cabin. I shall begin the pinafores tomorrow. I am so glad to have them to do ...

Off Queenstown, Friday, February 22nd 1861

My Dearest Etta,
We sailed, as you know, on Sunday the 17th, had a quiet night enough and Monday was tolerably calm

till the evening, when it began to blow; and during the night we had such a gale as is seldom met with. It *did* blow with a vengeance. The captain and all the officers were on deck all night; indeed, the former has not been in bed since we left Liverpool, such has been the weather.

… We had very rough weather during Tuesday and Wednesday, but still nothing remarkable, but yesterday morning it began to blow again, and for about six hours we had such a hurricane as no one on board ever saw before. To say that I never knew anything like it is nothing, but all the oldest sailors say a West Indian tornado was the only thing it was like.

Providentially it came by daylight; began about nine, and the worst was over by three. I could never give you the least idea of the force or roar of the wind, and some of the passengers who ventured on deck said the *Great Britain* big as she is, looked like a cockleshell among the waves, and that it seemed impossible but she must be buried in them.

She behaved admirably, took in very little water, and came up as stiff as possible after every roll. Several seas came on board, however; one broke into the saloon and thence into the cabins, one of which was three feet deep in water. The steward mopped and dipped it out in buckets. Some water got into our cabin, and, on going in to investigate, I found that one of my boxes was standing in a puddle; and remembering that the children's likeness was at the bottom of that very box. I determined, gale or no gale, to unpack it and get the picture out, which I did.

... When I came back to the saloon I found all the passengers grouped about, looking grave and somewhat frightened, expect one group of young men, who pretended to laugh over a game of cards, but who looked more alarmed than anyone when a harder squall than usual came on. I betook myself to a sofa at the end of the saloon to try and console some girls who were crying with terror, when the door opened and Captain Gray's cheerful face appeared. I asked him if the gale was abating, and he said yes, the worst was over and that he had never seen such a one before; and from then the wind went gradually down, leaving only a heavy swell, which had tumbled

173

us about all night and is now making this writing almost illegible.

Surry Hills, Sydney, May 15th 1861

My Dearest Etta,

… Somehow there was a good deal of stiffness and party feeling on board the ship. I hardly know how it arose, but half the people were not friendly with the other half. I enjoyed the voyage myself. I was always so wonderfully well; I never had a day's seasickness nor illness of any kind, and never was absent from a meal from the time I left Liverpool till I reached Sydney. It was a thing to be very thankful for; so many people were unwell at various times.

CHARLOTTE BRONTE, from Villette

I was not sick till long after we passed Margate, and deep was the pleasure I drank in with the sea breeze;

divine the delight I drew from the heaving Channel waves, from the sea-birds on their ridges, from the white sails on their dark distance, from the quiet yet beclouded sky, overhanging all. In my reverie, methought I saw the continent of Europe, like a wide dreamland, far away. Sunshine lay on it, making the long coast one line of gold; tiniest tracery of clustered town and snow-gleaming tower, of woods deep massed, of heights serrated, or smooth pasturage and veiny stream, embossed the metal-bright prospect. For background, spread a sky, solemn and dark blue, and – grand with imperial promise, soft with tints of enchantment – strode from north to south a God-bent bow, an arch of hope.

Cancel the whole of that, if you please, reader – or let it stand, and draw thence a moral – an alternative, text-hand copy.

Day-dreams are delusions of the demon.

Becoming excessively sick. I faltered down into the cabin.

VII

It seems to me: the sea and myself – and nothing else

When I was fifteen, when my mother was dead, I used to body-surf in the big waves of Makapu'u Point on the eastern coast of O'ahu. Once a lovely cove reached by a dirt path descending from a treacherous cliff, it is now a crowded beach with an acre of macadam parking lot with lunch wagons. But in 1963, it was still a secret place. One winter afternoon of high surf, when I would customarily have been using a fin – either a right or a left foot depending on one's inclination to break to the right or left of a wave – I loaned the fin to a friend who was also in the water. Makapu'u, with no lifeguard in those days, was known for its dangerous currents and tides. From earliest memory, we had been taught to abandon ourselves to the current should we ever

177

be swept away. If swimming parallel to shore in order to slip from the current proved ineffective, we were to allow ourselves to be carried out to sea, with the expectation that the current, in its circling way, would magnanimously hold you in its fierce arms, afloat, until it eventually returned you to the place from which you had been spirited. Assuming, that is, that the sharks did not take you, or you did not slip under the waves in exhaustion.

Tiny, uninhabited Rabbit Island was behind me on the horizon, then nothing but sea for thousands of miles. Tired soon by the big waves, perhaps because I was without a fin, I was resting, floating far enough from shore so that I was alone. I had turned to swim back to the surf when I realized that I was caught in the current. There was no one to see my struggle, no one to hear my cry over the roar of the waves. Against all wisdom, I fought it, unable to give myself to it, but it was useless; the current was too strong. I knew that I would not survive the long sweep out to sea. I would not be flung ashore with the returning tide, like Odysseus. I did not feel calm, or wonder, or acceptance, but terror.

I had already been pulled past the rocks that mark the headland to the bay when I felt a tug on my long braid. Then a rhythmic jerking as my body was pulled against the current. My nose and throat burned with salt water as I was dragged through the water. A boy was struggling to shore with my braid in his hand – I was too tired to help him, but let myself be pulled into shallow water – it was a luxurious feeling. He was a local boy, perhaps Hawaiian. For years, I dreamed about him, constructing a rather simple fantasy in which we fell in love and lived by the sea.

It is not surprising that many of my friends have died in the sea. In childhood, a young friend was killed by a great white shark while surfing at Lanika'i. My closest companion as a girl was Tommy Holmes, a scholarly waterman and authority on ocean canoes, who died young from a heart attack while steering a canoe off Waikiki. One friend disappeared while wind-surfing from O'ahu to Tahiti; another was lost in the Channel during a protest against the U.S. Navy's use of the island of Kaho'olawe for shelling practice. As I have been saved from drowning, I have saved others. I have buried friends at sea, a rather laborious and sometimes humorous (the beloved's ashes in one's eyes and mouth) task given that it is illegal in Hawaiian waters without a permit. It is traditional after spewing the ashes or lowering the corpse into the sea for the mourners to jump into the ocean and swim to shore. That enterprise – long distances, heavy seas, too much alcohol – has led to its own terrors and delights.

In 1993 I wrote in my novel *Sleeping Beauties* of a young woman, Clio, and her Aunt Emma, descendants of an early missionary family. Clio is in love with a Hawaiian named Henry. In the book, the three of them take a small boat to the island of Kaho'olawe, off the coast of Maui, to join a demonstration against the decades-long use of the island by the United States military as a bombing site.

> The boat was very small, as he had said.
> The life preservers were stuffed beneath
> the console. There was a radio so that
> Henry could talk to the other boats. His

cousin Leroy was on a blue sampan. One of the fishing boats had been chartered by the Human Reactor, who had come from Hiroshima after all.

The Coast Guard had dispatched a cutter and it was so close that Clio could see the faces of the young sailors as they watched idly from the sides. They looked sunburned and a little bored.

The island of Kaho'olawe, bare of vegetation, disappeared with each new sweep of water, and Clio, like the sailors, wondered why they were there.

Emma stood at the wheel with Henry. "All cultures end eventually, Henry," she shouted, turning to smile at Clio.

Henry, intent on keep the small boat steady, did not answer. Emma turned again to Clio and beckoned to her with a gesture that seemed to take in the sky and bleak Kaho'olawe, and even the pink-faced, sullen boys on the cutter.

"I wonder what a Human Reactor looks like?" Emma called gaily to Clio.

Clio looked at her, surprised by her sudden anger at Emma. She wondered for a moment if she were jealous. Perhaps she did not wish to share Henry, the presence of Henry, even with Emma. But she knew that it was not jealousy. It was Emma's change of heart. It was an insult to Clio, who had lived in her service for years. She believes that all the time in the world is ahead of her, thought Clio, and I believe that all time is behind me.

Another boat came alongside. An old Hawaiian charter captain was at the wheel, a Kona fisherman named Pupule.

He waved to Henry.

Henry waved back at him.

In the front of Pupule's boat stood a small Japanese man in a yellow slicker and black gloves. He, too, waved.

Emma looked at him, then turned to

Clio, smiling in amusement. "Do you think he wears that oilskin to contain his rays?"

Clio smiled and nodded, distracted. She had been watching the cutter, suddenly near enough to be either purposeful or careless. Henry, too, had noticed the closeness of the boat. She wondered if the Coast Guard were preparing to lower sailors into their boat. Perhaps they were going to be arrested.

And then the Coast Guard boat rammed them from behind.

With a startled smile, Emma stumbled against the rail. She turned to Clio, and put out her hand, and fell into the sea.

Henry grabbed a rope from the deck, and a life preserver, and pointing off the bow, pushed the line and the vest into Clio's outstretched hands.

Clio could see driftwood and seaweed, foam and wrack, all with sudden clarity, but she could not see Emma.

The boat rolled from side to side. Henry idled the engine, fearful of hitting Emma, or the other boats, rocking, too, in confusion. He turned the boat in slow, small circles. On the other boat, Pupule climbed to the fishing tower. His boat swayed so wildly that his outrigger poles seemed to touch the sea. The man in the yellow coat huddled in the cabin.

A rescue boat was lowered from the cutter. It too roiled in the rough sea, and the helmsman raced the engine trying to outrun a swell, making a sudden deep wake that rushed upon the smaller boats. A wave washed over them, and Clio was swept into the sea.

The waves broke without regret, without pleasure. Salt burned in her nose and throat. She lay on her back and tried to breathe, tried to find the bright sky and black Kaho'olawe. The sea lifted her high, and dropped her with a roar.

Someone called her name.

It is my grandfather, she thought. My grandfather who drowned one winter evening of rapture of the deep.

But it was not her grandfather.

It is Uncle McCully who drowned in a tidal wave looking for Mamie.

But it was not them.

She could hear the women and the unheeding children and the reckless warriors and fishermen, lost at sea, all of them calling to her,

But she was wrong. It was none of these. It was Henry. It was Henry, calling her name.

She fought hard against the water god. When the sailors tried to pull her into their boat, she resisted with such ferocity that she broke her collarbone in the struggle. She thought that she was bodysurfing with the Hawaiian boys at Makapu'u Point. "Where is my fin?" she

185

asked. "I lost my fin." The young sailors finally lied to her, telling her they had her fin in the boat. Only then did Clio stop struggling and allow them to lift her from the lamenting sea.

Emma was taken by the god as she had known she would be were he ever given the chance, and her body, because of this, was never recovered.

I used to flatter myself that I lived only on islands – Manhattan and England to name just two – but there are too many islands in the world and too many people living on them to make any mystical claims. I've spent my life by the sea, but so have millions of others. To my regret (what to do?), I am less courageous in the sea than I once was – my friends would have said that I was reckless as a girl – and there are no more romantic rescues. My life, longer now, still has not flashed before my eyes in a moment of drowning, but there is time. I take less chances, I swim less far, I no longer swim alone at night. I am no longer without fear. I used to think that it was a sign of my growing wisdom, but it is really a sign of my fading strength. When I was body-surfing last Christmas, I injured my neck. Still, I cannot renounce the ocean. I'd like my body to be given to the sea when I am dead, a gesture that is almost impossible these days for reasons of public safety. I sometimes wonder what it is like to drown.

There were two times when I came close to losing my virginity, appropriately for an island girl, in the sea, once when I was nineteen and again when I was twenty. The first time was at Hanalei on the north shore of Kaua'i, on a moonless night, in about fourteen inches of water, I was on my back, propped on my elbows, my face now and than washed by a wave. I was relieved, in the end, that the enterprise was abandoned, in part because the sea robbed me of the vaginal lubrication necessary for such an occasion, and the cool water did not avail my seducer of his full powers.

The second time was in the warmer waters of the Bay of Mexico. Surrounded by suitably romantic phosphoresence, little fishes nibbling at my heels, this attempt was thwarted by the sudden presence of a large black shape visible behind the head of my beloved, which nudged him in the back, thus ending the exercise. If it is possible to be trampled in water, I was. The next morning I saw the piles of roughly-buried eggs and clumsy, wavering tracks that signified the arrival on the island of turtles to lay their eggs, a symmetry of biology that possessed a pleasant irony.

Once I left the islands, as a young woman, my life in the ocean was ended. The Atlantic Ocean could not compare to my southern seas, although the Mediterranean and the Adriatic, the Aegean, the Sea of Cortes and the Indian Ocean were ravishing substitutes. The sea became a matter of summer holidays, and resorts out of season. Never the same. And I was never the same for it.

Acknowledgments

The author is indebted to the following publishers for permission to quote from their publications:

I

Daniel Defoe, from *The Life and Strange Surprising Adventures of Robinson Crusoe,* The Heritage Press, New York, 1930;

John Fiske, *The Discovery of America,* Vol. 1, Houghton Mifflin and Company, Boston, 1893;

"Song" first appeared in *Last of the Seris*. Copyright © 1939 by Dane Coolidge and Mary Roberts

II

Herman Melville, *Moby Dick,* R. R. Donnelley Sons
Company, New York, 1930;

Charles Darwin, *The Voyage of the Beagle,* Doubleday
& Company, Inc., New York, 1962;

Julian Corbett, from *Sir Francis Drake,* MacMillan
and Co., London, 1901;

Joseph Conrad, *Typhoon and Other Stories,* Random
House, New York, 2003;

Herodotus, from *The History,* translated by D.

Grene, copyright the University of Chicago, 1987, reprinted by permission of the publisher.

III

Sir James George Frazer, from *The Golden Bough* reprinted by permission of the Master and Fellows of Trinity College, Cambridge;

Ford Madox Ford, from *Joseph Conrad,* copyright The Ecco Press, 1989, New York, reprinted with permission of David Higham Associates Limited, London;

Thomas Mann, from *Death in Venice,* copyright Dover Publications, 1995, reprinted by permission of the publisher;

Walt Whitman, from *Poetry and Prose,* The Library of America, 1982, New York, reprinted with permission of the publisher;

IV

D. H. Lawrence, from *The Complete Poems.* Ware, Herts. 1994;

Pliny the Younger, from *Letters* Volume II. Translated by William Melmoth; revised by W. M. L. Hutchinson. London 1915;

Anonymous, from *The New Oxford Book of Irish Verse,* edited with translations by Thomas Kinsella. Oxford and New York 1986.

V

Emily Dickinson, from *The Poems of Emily Dickinson.* London 1933;

Excerpt from *The Waves* by Virginia Woolf, copyright © 1931 by Harcourt, Inc. and renewed 1959 by Leonard Woolf, reprinted by permission of Harcourt, Inc.;

HM Kalakaua, King of Hawai'i, from *The Legends and Myths of Hawai'i.* Honolulu 1990;

John Keats, from *The Complete Poems,* Random House, New York, 1951;

Wilkie Collins, from *The Moonstone,* Penguin, London, 1968;

Robert Louis Stevenson, from *Treasure Island,* Cassell and Company, London, 1883;

Henry David Thoreau, from *Henry David Thoreau: A Week, Walden, Maine Woods, Cape Cod,* The Library of America, 1985, New York, reprinted with permission of the publisher;

Anton Chekhov, from *Notebook,* B. W. Huebsch, New York, 1921;

Washington Irving, from *The Sketch Book of Geoffrey Crayon, Gent.,* G. P. Putnam, 1848, New York, reprinted with permission of the publisher.

VI

D. H. Lawrence, from The *Letters of D H Lawrence*
Volume IV. Edited by Warren Roberts, James T.
Boulton and Elizabeth Mansfield. Cambridge University
Press 1987, reprinted by permission of the publisher;

Isabella Bird, from *Six Months in the Sandwich Islands,*
copyright Mutual Publishing, Honolulu, 1998,
reprinted by permission of the publisher;

Hesiod, from *Works and Days,* in *The Homeric Hymns
and Homerica.* Translated by Hugh G. Evelyn-White.
London 1914;

Rachel Henning, from *The Letters of Rachel Henning,*
edited by David Adams, Penguin, 1969, reprinted
by permission of HarperCollins Publishers;

Charlotte Brontë, from *Villette,* J.M. Dent & Sons
Ltd., London, 1853.